This book is dedicated to Martin's father-in-law
— Alfred William Barber

CONTENTS

ACKNOWLEDGEMENTS

May I please thank all the members of the Hillier family and the staff of
Hillier Nurseries; Edward Roberts; Winchester Museum Services; and
Hampshire County Records Office — and so many others for all their help
and kindness. — M.D.

©

M. Drew

First published: February, 1992

Compton — its church and school

Gordon Martin Carter Drew, to be known, for all time, simply as Martin, died as he had lived — unashamedly true to his birth.

Arrogance and pretentiousness would have slipped from his shoulders, as a cloak without ties, from a warrior in battle. He lived by the unwritten code of the countryside and served it with honour. A country boy, a village lad and that village was Compton, near Winchester.

He was caught up in the magical web of rural life and found it to be all embracing. Very few of those born into similar situations during the early part of this century ever completely extricated themselves from the web. It was as though the fibres were woven into their future and brought about a completeness, a belonging that had such a lasting effect.

It was a tight knit community, limiting, restricting and more often than not, unbending but it was the continuity, the wonderful comforting familiarity knowing that spring would follow winter as surely as night follows day. That the sun would rise and would as surely set.

Relying on each other cemented a strength that upheld and uplifted, and was the true backbone of this small village. It was as a precious jewel, uncut and unspoiled in its original setting.

The true beauty of village life is the product of years, in the same way that peat can only be hewn from the bowels of the earth after years of natural formation. There is nothing instant in either case.

The village scene is created by the day to day toil of ordinary folk. Generations of the same families content to work on the farms and in the big houses, not to amass great wealth, but in order to support their families.

In so doing, they left a fortune. A fortune we have all inherited in the village life we enjoy today. Let us all hope, indeed pray, that it will never be spoiled. That the humility they showed may linger in the countryside for all time.

Before too long, Martin was to be born into the life of this Hampshire village, to play his part in its history — to be part of the school and of the church. But the village had more years to spend first.

Opposite: Martin Drew in 'his' greenhouse at Braishfield. It was here that he coaxed his show plants into giving that little bit extra with which to delight the public.

Ernie and Kate Drew on their wedding day.

He was destined to be the only child of Kate and Ernie Drew. Their union embracing a wider union of children brought up in neighbouring villages, in the shadow of their mother churches but within the all embracing diocese of Winchester and its beautiful Cathedral.

Ernie Drew was a miller living in the village of Twyford when he courted and married Kate, who was in service at Compton where she lived with her parents, five sisters and four brothers at Fishing Cottage.

Their marriage ceremony took place in Compton Church on 22nd December, 1923 and was performed by the Rector, John Blackett.

It was the beginning of a lifetime's association with Compton Church, for this newly married young couple.

Their life style was little different from that of their contemporaries. Money was short and life was hard but without visible alternatives with which to compare, it was not seen as such. It was their lot in life and they bore the comparative poverty with fortitude and complete acceptance.

Above: Twyford Church which Ernest Drew attended in his youth. Below: Compton Church where he married Kate Carter and which was to play a prominent part in their lives.

They served with gratitude the folk in the big houses. 'Sir' and 'Madam' were an integral part of their language. The men touched their forelock or doffed their caps with all the naturalness of a babe sucking his thumb. To question such an act would be a betrayal of their class. Their place on the ladder of life was secure and strong. They had no wish to climb or to undermine those in authority for to do so would weaken their very foundations and their lives would crumble.

It never occurred to them to do other than strive to please the Master or Mistress of the house who afforded them their fragile independence.

So Kate and Ernie with neither thought nor hope of a home of their own, moved thankfully into Fishing Cottage with Kate's parents.

Her father, Isaac, was a hard man. His authority at home, unquestioned. His word was law and the word compromise unknown to him. His wife, Caroline, and their ten children never sought to undermine this power. Indeed it was their security for there could be no measure of independence outside the framework of their family life.

Below: Fishing Cottage (now called Itchen Cottage) – the home of Isaac Carter and his wife, who had ten children.

Isaac and Caroline Carter.

It is intriguing to wonder whether Isaac felt as secure in his God-given role as he would have them believe or was it mere mimicry of his daily work situation when he was as the child who questioned not the hand that fed him.

The farmer, Edward Lyne, for whom Isaac toiled long and hard, held little understanding of the problems of his employees. He purchased their labour unhindered by family responsibility and so Isaac became adept at relegating his ever increasing family to the identical position he held in his employment. To do otherwise would be to teeter on the edge of an abyss and Isaac was not about to do that. Self-preservation was engraved across his soul.

Overleaf: Compton circa 100 years ago.

9

Compton

Rectory

All Saints' Ch.

(Rectory)

School

Post Office

Grave Yard

Smithy

Compton Farm

Place Lane

BARN

43
26·066

44
3·156

42
2·401

41
4·303

40
·612

39
1·929

38
3·015

37
·094

36
·604

35
·475

34
·378

33
1·114

32
·751

31
1·744

69
34·126

67
·967

B.M. 195·1

·135

·54

·81

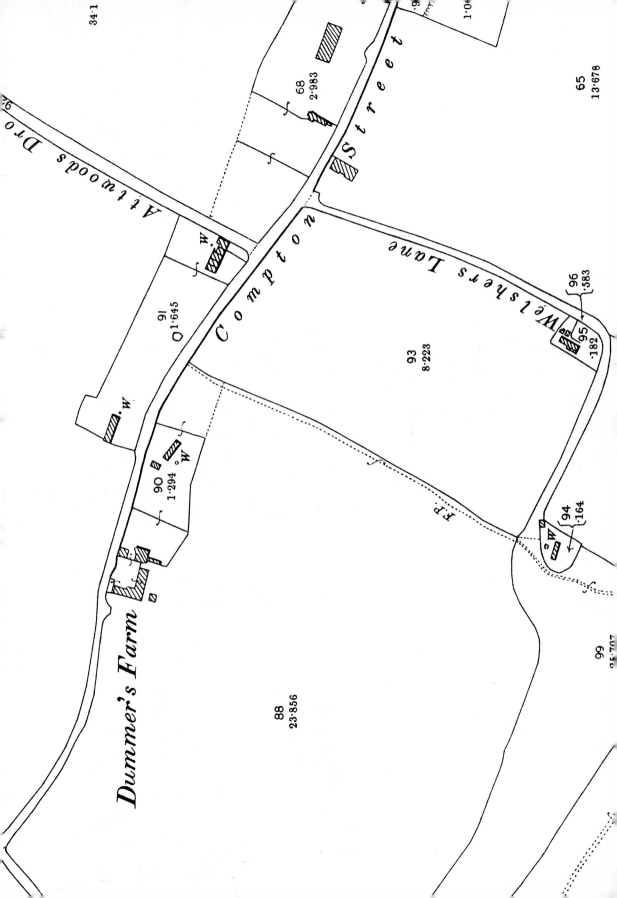

The School Log Book

When Kate was born in 1898, Compton village had 480 people. Its population was rising fast — with Isaac having played no little part in this!

As Compton set off into the 20th century, Edward Lyne gave up the tenancy of Compton Farm and it was taken over by James Stratton and his step-son, Wilfred Godwin, who many years later provided the name for the close just off Compton Street. Godwin's Field now has five bungalows built and fitted, with the older generation of Compton folk in mind.

It was during the following years that an important event took place, that involved the whole village. The church was, by now, much too small for the fast growing community and one has to remember that all parishioners regularly worshipped on Sundays. It was, therefore, decided to enlarge it and work began during the month of May, 1905 and was completed within a few months. Such a mammoth task in so short a time would be unthinkable today. There was concerted effort and unwavering dedication by all Parishioners, rich and poor alike, to raising the necessary money for their church. And, of course, it *was* their church, for it featured so largely in their daily lives.

The church and school were unhindered in their influence on Compton village. Outside agencies were not to creep in until much later to vie for the time and interest in these busy people. Meanwhile, the school provided the only education for most of the children although it often took second place to haymaking, golf and shooting!

The following extracts from the school log book paint the picture of Compton school days at the turn of the century:

1891 — March 2nd

First entry made, as no log book has been required in this school before.

Began new registers with 27 scholars on books.

April 16th

Copy of the Report of Her Majesty's Inspectors.

The children are well behaved and have good manners. In point of attainment the two lower standards do well, but in the fourth and fifth standard both spelling and arithmetic are very defective and the latter subject is also weak in the third standard. Care should be taken that the children understand the principles of the rules they learn.

The attendance of the older boys seems to be remarkably irregular, though this may be partly due to the prevalence of an epidemic.

The needlework is creditable. Better results in the higher standards will be expected as a condition of the renewal of a certificate of efficiency.

Signed   Charles Wickham Rector   Annie A. Dedmen
              (Correspondent of the School)   (Schoolmistress)

Children beside the fence that now borders the gardens of the homes of Sid and Hazel Lowe and Tony and Jenny Cave-Penny.

1896 — November 6th

Richard Hunt received six strokes on the hand for insubordination and rudeness to the Assistant Mistress during the absence of Mistress yesterday.

November 24th

Fred Wakley received one stroke of the cane on each hand, for disobedience.

November 27th

Five boys who brought their dinners to school went off to play on the Downs and did not return to school till 1.50 instead of 1.30. Some of them had been warned before of a like offence, therefore they were all caned as follows:

R. Hunt and W. Steele	— six strokes
A. Hand	— four strokes
R. Barnes and Al Hand	— two strokes

December 7th

Fred Wakley received two strokes of the cane for tearing a geography book.

December 14th

Two families are absent with measles. Mr. Woodman visited. He proposed to close the school at once to prevent the spread of measles.

1897 — January 25th

Owing to the measles having spread, school could not be opened until today. The children who have returned seem to have forgotten most of their work.

February 7th

Walter Steele received four strokes of the cane for disobedience; his sister one, for urging him to disobey.

February 17th

Leonard Smith received two strokes of the cane for idleness and inattention.

March 11th

A great number of boys absent having gone to golf (they carried the players' clubs).

March 15th

Leonard Smith received four strokes of the cane for disobedience and defiance.

March 18th

Six of the bigger boys have again gone to golf.

March 23rd

William Steele, Chas. Wilmot and Leonard Smith each received three and Richard Hunt two strokes of the cane for bad conduct yesterday.

Mrs. Steele alleged that William's thumb was dislocated by this punishment. His work was done as usual during the morning. Rev. C. Wickham visited to inspect the thumb, finding it quite lissom.

Copy of Government Report, 1897

An improvement is shown in the writing and the reading is fair, but arithmetic will need much attention, particularly in the second and fifth standards. Geography is fair, and needlework is fairly good. The discipline is satisfactory. The room is now very full, 62 being present on the day of examination. The provision of a classroom for the infants may be recommended, and better cloakroom accommodation is required.

Care should be taken to prevent overcrowding and the question of providing additional classroom and cloakroom accommodation should be considered.

The managers attention is directed to article 85(a) of the code, and to the enclosed Form 69.

Signed   Charles Wickham
Staff for 1897-8
         Grace Mary Atkins   Certificated Mistress
         Mary Poulter

May 27th

Being Ascension Day, the children received scripture lesson, attended church and had holiday in the afternoon. Registers not marked all day.

May 28th

School assembled at 1 p.m. in the afternoon and dismissed at 3.15 p.m. for school cleaning.

Rev. C. Wickham visited and taught scripture (this visit by the Rector for scripture lesson was a frequent occurrence).

June 14th

Following the one week Whitsuntide vacation, school re-opened this morning. Only two boys present in upper standard.

June 14th

Received 2¾lb wool; 9 yds. Print; 2 doz. yds. Calico; 6 yds. Holland; 10 yds. Apron Linen.

June 25th

The attendance of boys is very poor, as they are being employed on the farms. (Martin's uncle was one of these.)

July 5th

Robert Barnes, Herbert Spurdle, Arthur Hand and James Bradley have all been punished for throwing stones and the other children warned as there are several windows broken.

July 12th

Received from London—

27 maps (outline); 7 doz. Exercise Books; 8½ doz Copy-Books; ½ doz. Reading Books St. 4; 1½ doz. Readers St. 5; 1½ doz. Slates; 1½ doz. Geography Books; 1 Box Chalk; 1 set Drg. Sheets; 1 doz. Inf. Readers; 4 doz. Drg. Books.

July 30th

Rev. C. Wickham visited and taught scripture. At 12 o'clock today the Harvest Holidays commence — four weeks.

August 30th

School re-opened this morning.

August 31st

Rev. C. Wickham visited. The Managers recommend that no new children be admitted from Shawford, as there is room for them at Twyford and we are rather crowded.

September 15th

Ethel Smith received four strokes of the cane for laziness in the arithmetic lesson.

September 20th

Attendance Officer visited.

Received an insulting note from Mrs. Allen, in consequence of Mabel having been degraded to st. 4 for arithmetic. Her abilities and attendance combined made this necessary.

September 23rd

Very poor attendance, there being a sale of Mr. Pearson's farm stock, all the children from his farm have been absent.

October 11th

Thirteen children have left during the last fortnight owing to changes at the farms.

November 3rd

Examined the first class infants. The reading only was satisfactory; the other work is very crude.

November 5th

Rev. C. Wickham visited and taught scripture. Three boys have gone with some sportsmen to shoot, instead of coming to school.

December 2nd

Four boys and a girl were caned for disorderly conduct and disobedience to the mistress on the road home from school. Leonard Smith, the ringleader refused to hold out his hand as his mother had told him he could do as he liked out of school.

December 17th

Harry Carter, infant, was caned for stubborn behaviour to his teacher (he was Martin's uncle).

1898 — January 31st

Received notice of the payment of the Special Aid Grant. A 'grant of £7 is made for providing a monitor or pupil-teacher, and new books'.

January 31st

Needlework and drawing lessons were taken in the afternoon instead of singing, as the mistress had a bad headache.

February 23rd

No school was held today, as it was Ash Wednesday. A scripture lesson was given, and then all but the babies were taken to church.

March 8th

Headmistress has been absent from her duties for four days, suffering from a severe attack of influenza — during which time she has been sent for to return twice, by the Rev. C. Wickham, chairman of the Committee of Managers.

Head-mistress resigns

April 29th

Today I resign my charge of this school having obtained an appointment nearer London.   Grace M. Atkins.

With the change of Headmistress comes a change in log book reporting notably an absence of caning although this practice undoubtedly still took place.

May 5th

I, Alice Florence Clarke, take charge as Headmistress today.

July 18th

Admitted Gladys Carter (Martin's aunt who was just three years old, having been born on 7th June 1895. She wanted to go to school with her brothers and sisters).

September 2nd

Several children have not yet returned. Elsie and Harry Carter absent as they are suffering from ringworms (Martin's aunt and uncle).

September 23rd

Arthur Hand has been expelled for swearing and afterwards very indecent behaviour. Rev. C. Wickham has approved this expulsion.

October 17th

Elsie and Annie Carter are absent with ringworms (two more of Martin's aunts).

(Over the next six weeks many of the children were absent from school because of ringworm.)

1899 — February 1st

Older boys absent today being out with a gentlemen's shooting party.

March 22nd

Attendance very bad, especially in upper standards — only *six* present in standards III, IV, V, VI boys and girls.

June 7th

A holiday will be given tomorrow, as a general holiday will be given in Winchester for the visit of his R.H. Prince of Wales.

June 13th

Permission given to Percy Mitchell to help with the hay making.

James Bradley, Albert Edwards and Harry Carter (Martin's uncle) absent — carrying for golf, after being forbidden.

July 13th

Copy of H.M. Inspectors Report.

Mixed School — The school is under able instruction and the children appear to be making good progress. But the shape of the room and the necessarily inconvenient arrangement of desks makes the teachers' task a difficult one. A decision should be arrived at as the best way of supplying the required accommodation either by enlarging the existing site and building or by building a new school in a better position.

Infants Class — The infants are satisfactorily taught. The registers must be tested by the Managers at least once a quarter at irregular intervals as required by paragraph six of Appendix II of instructions to inspectors. Attention is directed to Article 85(d) of the code. My Lords will be glad to know what the Managers have decided upon with regard to providing suitable accommodation for the infants. Unless this is done, it may be necessary to withhold the grant for their attendance and pay on those of the older children only (Article 98).

September 10th

Duties resumed this morning in the Shawford Hall. No Silkstead children present owing to the outbreak of fever there.

September 29th

Attendance still worse today — all elder boys absent carrying for golf.

October 9th

Annie Alexander has returned this morning — she has only made *four* attendances since July 24th.

1900 — January 19th

Attendance has been very bad this week. *Fifteen* children absent all the week while five others only came one day and several others were very irregular.

March 12th

Admitted George Carter — infant (Martin's uncle).

May 1st

A holiday given today being May Day.

May 24th

Ascension Day — a holiday given.

July 23rd

Lily Jetton absent since June 23rd with ringworm. Bessie Pitters absent with bad throat and Alfred Steele through falling on a scythe and badly cutting his leg.

October 2nd

Dr. Roberts visited and looked at several of the children's throats.

October 26th

Three boys in stan. III employed as beaters today.

1901 — February 5th

Owing to a heavy fall of snow — very poor attendance.

February 12th

Captain Forrest visited and spoke to children about irregular attendance.

February 20th

Today being Ash Wednesday a whole holiday given.

March 4th

Numbers very bad owing to whooping cough.

March 25th

Harry and Annie Carter returned today, also Bessie and William Wakley.

Population of Compton 260

Plan of proposed additions at Compton School

Scale ½ inch to the foot

Wm Coles & Son

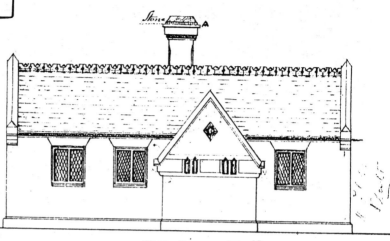

Elevation. North

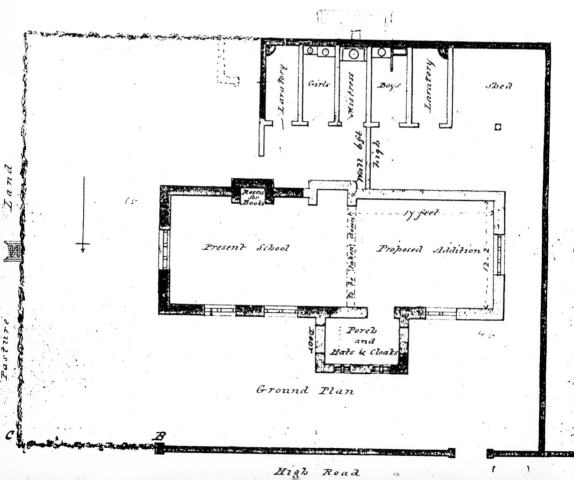

Pasture Land

Lavatory · Girls · Mistress · Boys · Lavatory · Shed

Recess for Books

Present School

Proposed Addition

17 feet

12. 2

15

Door

Porch
and
Hats & Cloaks

Church Yard

Ground Plan

C   B

High Road

The Golf Pavilion on Shawford Downs where many, many boys played truant from Compton School to caddy for golfers.

Martin's uncles were involved in playing truant in order to earn a little money for carrying golf clubs.

Mr. Burton mowed all the greens of the Shawford Golf Club during Martin's school days.

April 25th

Diocesan inspection in religious knowledge takes place tomorrow.

Copy of Report of Religious Instruction

	Stans II-V	Stan I & Infants
Old Test.	very good	very good
New Test.	very good	very good
Catechism	very good	good
Prayer Bk	good	—
Repetition	very good	very good
Writing	very fairly good	—

General Remarks

The school is well taught — the tone and discipline are good, the private prayers well known and singing bright.

Good and useful work is being carried on. The elder children did well in all their subjects. In writing, however, two at least did not do the work set them.

The infants are taught to use their intelligence. Some scripture pictures would be a great help to the teacher.

June 17th

Admitted Kate Carter — infant (Martin's mother) and Charles Eldridge.

July 15th

Stands II and V taken for walk onto the Downs and given lesson on the surrounding country — also geographical definitions.

September 17th

Harry Carter (Martin's uncle) and James Bradley have come in this week.

September 20th

Elsie Carter (Martin's aunt) has left this week.

November 19th

Girls in stands. IV and V brought garments to receive lessons in mending this week.

1902 — March 19th

School closed today for the funeral of the Rev. C. Wickham.

April 18th

Usual routine this week. The school correspondent, Captain Forrest, visited this morning and spoke to the children about irregular attendance. Several children were away then.

May 2nd

Rev. and Mrs. Blake visited on Monday afternoon.

('The Rector visited and took scripture' were the main entries in the log book at this time with the usual recorded holidays and days off for May Day, Ascension Day and so on.)

1903 — July 30th

Mrs. Blake (Rector's wife) visited this morning and gave prizes to several children for regular attendance.

Harvest holidays commence this afternoon.

September 4th

School re-opened on Monday morning. Attendance very poor indeed all this week, owing chiefly to the late harvest. So many of the elder children being employed now as the weather is good.

November 4th

Received letter from Dr. Roberts saying that all Silkstead children also Butchers (three) of New Barn were not to come to school this week owing to a case of scarlet fever at Spreadburys.

1904 — July 11th
Copy of Government Report

Mixed School
The teaching is good and careful but the children are heavy and inert and this makes the work very difficult.

The drawing and needlework were good and the written work was well done but mental effort was sadly lacking.

The children need much rousing.

Infant Class
The infants are kindly treated and are satisfactorily taught.

The diamond window frames obstruct much light.

Signed   Cecil H. Cooper
            Rector
Staff for 1904
            A. F. Clarke   Certificated Mistress
            M. Poulter   Art 68

November 11th
Attendance very poor this week again. *Seventeen* children absent this afternoon.

November 14th
Maud Lucas has returned this morning after an absence of eight weeks.

November 18th
Sarah Broad returned after being absent for *nine* weeks.

1905 — March 14th
Copy of Report made by H.M. Inspector.

Mixed Department and Infants Class
Michaelmas changes and much sickness have been hindrances during the past year but the mechanical work is again well done, and mental power and self effort are being gradually developed.

A school clock is needed (this simple statement by the Inspector, was to be another thread yet to be woven into Martin's future).

The infants class is being creditably taught, but the light in their room is still marred by the diamond-shaped window frames.

Staff
            Mary Poulter   Art 68
            Alice Florence Clarke   Certificated Mistress
Signed   Cecil H. H. Cooper
            Rector of Compton

Working on the church extensions – 1905.

June 9th

School broke up this morning for Whitsuntide holiday — fortnight being given to allow elder boys to work during hay making.

July 14th

Frances Abraham has been absent since Tuesday morning when her mother came in and rudely fetched her out while kept in from play, when kept in to do work again that had been very badly done.

September 1st

Ernest Lucas and William Broad absent, working for Mr. Godwin.

October 31st

Half holiday given this afternoon for the consecration of the additions made to the old church also on Wednesday morning, November 1st.

In 1905, Compton Church was enlarged to accommodate the increased congregation. Above: the new; below: the old interior.

1906 — May 11th

Taken off the name of Annie Carter, having been through the standards and now left school. (Martin's aunt, who before long was to leave Compton village without trace.)

June 8th

Closed this morning for two weeks' holiday, given now instead of at Whitsuntide to allow elder boys to help with the hay making.

1907 — September 4th

Attendance very poor so far — all the elder boys still employed in the harvest fields.

1908 — October 12th

Two cases of diphtheria have broken out and several other cases of ailing children are reported — only 29 present this morning and 28 this afternoon.

1909 — September 6th

Duties resumed this morning with very poor number. No Silkstead or New Barn children present owing to farmer employing boys for harvest work.

Copy of Report by H.M. Inspector — December 2nd

This little school, though it suffers from continual changes produces, on the whole, good results. The mistress works well and sensibly and is endeavouring to train her children in habits of self-reliance.

The answering is good though hardly as general as it used to be but it seems that the Head Teacher is attempting too much.

She teaches all the children above the infants herself leaving to the assistant only a handful of little children.

The supplementary teacher must take and be responsible for the efficient teaching of more children than this, including standard I otherwise it may be impossible to continue to recognise her.

Staff

	Mary Poulter	Supp. T
	Alice F. Clarke	Cert. T
Signed	C. R. Durham	Rector

1910 — May 19th

Whole holiday tomorrow being the late King's funeral.

1911 — December 13th

Registers not marked this moring as only 18 children came and many of those were very wet. The Rector came and we therefore decided to send them home again to remove their damp boots and clothing.

Compton Church and Compton School, with the children lined up in the playground presumably to have their photograph taken at the beginning of the century.

Unmentionable Daughter?

When the time came for James Stratton to retire, Farmer Godwin shouldered the responsibility of providing the livelihood of so many in the area, thereby enabling Isaac to execute the task of seeing his family well fed, shod and mindful of God's teaching until they could be placed in suitable employment, to be followed by convenient marriages.

There remains one child of which the writers have been unable to trace — Annie, known to the family as Nancy or Nance because of Caroline Carter's custom of bestowing nicknames on her children. For example, Kate was called Kit.

As the school log book confirms, Annie was admitted to Compton School on 15th October, 1896 and left ten uneventful years later; soon to be banished from Compton by her father, Isaac.

Her brothers and sisters were forbidden to mention her name ever again, and mindful (or fearful?) of their father, acquiescence was assured. So this sad young girl left her home, parents, brothers and sisters, for what reason and for what destination nobody knows.

Newspaper cutting 1925 – Hunt balls.

HUNT AND COUNTY BALLS.

We publish below a list of forthcoming hunt and county balls. The list will be revised and repeated on successive Mondays until the end of the year :—

NOVEMBER 19.—North Northumberland Hunt Ball, Haggerston Castle.

DECEMBER 7.—The Radcliffe Infirmary and Oxfordshire County Ball, Town Hall, Oxford (Clifford Essex Band).

DECEMBER 15.—Wylye Valley Hunt Ball, Town Hall, Warminster (Clifford Essex Band).

DECEMBER 17.—Montgomeryshire County Ball (Newman's Band).

DECEMBER 18.—The Blankney Hunt Ball, Assembly Rooms, Lincoln, 10 p.m. ; the Atherstone Hunt Ball, Newnham Paddox ; North Staffordshire Hunt Ball, Maer Hall, near Newcastle, Staffs.

DECEMBER 21.—Morpeth Hunt Ball.

DECEMBER 22.—South Notts Hunt Ball, The Palais-de-Danse, Nottingham.

DECEMBER 29.—The Isle of Wight Hunt Ball, Ryde Town Hall (Newman's Band).

DECEMBER 30.—The Tiverton Hunt Ball ; Royal Berkshire Hospital Ball, Town Hall, Reading ; Cheshire County Assembly, Royal George Hotel, Knutsford.

JANUARY 1.—Blackmore Vale Hunt Ball, Sherborne ; West Kent Hunt Ball ; Albrighton Hunt Ball ; Devon and Somerset Staghounds Hunt Ball, Metropole Hotel, Minehead ; Hampshire County Ball, Guildhall, Winchester ; Royal West Sussex Hospital Ball, Assembly Rooms, Chichester (Clifford Essex Band). Essex Union Hunt Ball, Shire Hall, Chelmsford ; Llangibby Hunt Ball, Newport, Monmouthshire (Clifford Essex Band).

JANUARY 4.—High Peak Hunt Ball, Buxton (Conri Tait's Band).

JANUARY 5.—South and West Wilts Hunt Ball ; Buckingham County Ball, Stowe School ; Chester Royal Infirmary Ball, Grosvenor Hotel, Chester. Mendip Hunt Ball, Guildhall, Wells (Clifford Essex Band) ; Brecon Hunt Ball, The Castle Hotel, Brecon (Newman's Band).

JANUARY 6.—Stamford Infirmary Ball, Assembly Rooms, Stamford ; York Fancy Dress Ball. The Assembly Rooms (Vassie and his No. 1 Band).

JANUARY 7.—The Pytchley Hunt Ball ; Westmorland County Ball, Town Hall, Kendal ; Suffolk County Ball, the Athenæum, Bury St. Edmunds ; the Hertford County Ball, Town Hall, Hertford.

JANUARY 8.—Dorset Hunt Ball, the Corn Exchange, Dorchester ; the New Forest Spinsters' Ball, Morant Hall, Brockenhurst ; the Newark Hospital and Dispensary Ball, Town Hall, Newark ; Mid-Kent Stag Hounds Hunt Ball, Corn Exchange, Maidstone.

JANUARY 11.—Monmouthshire Hunt Ball, the Rolls Hall, Monmouth ; the Berkeley and Ledbury Hunt Ball, Guildhall, Gloucester.

JANUARY 12.—The Craven Hunt Club Ball, Corn Exchange, Newbury ; Devon County Ball (Newman's Band) ; Eridge Hunt Ball, the Pump Room, Tunbridge Wells ; the Worcestershire Hunt Club Ball, the Shirehall, Worcester.

JANUARY 13.—The V.W.H. (Earl Bathurst's) Hunt Ball, Bingham Hall, Cirencester.

JANUARY 14.—Earl Fitzwilliam's (Grove) Hunt Ball, Town Hall, Retford ; Grantham Hospital Ball.

JANUARY 21.—Avon Vale Hunt Ball, Town Hall, Trowbridge (Clifford Essex Band) ; the United Counties Hunt Ball, Market Harborough.

JANUARY 22.—The Cambridgeshire County Ball, Guildhall, Cambridge ; the Avon Vale Farmers' Ball.

FEBRUARY 5.—The Cottesmore Hunt Ball, Oakham.

The old church and churchyard of St. Mary-in-Arden at Market Harborough, after being derelict for more than a century, have lately been put into order with the idea of again holding services in the church. On Saturday they were formally reopened by the Bishop of Leicester. Some parts of the church date back to 1066,

Martin and England of the 1920s!

Because of their social upbringing Kate and Ernie thought it natural to live with Kate's parents.

To this background they came came after their marriage and they soon settled down to hard work in the beautiful countryside. A simple life that brought fulfilment and quiet contentment.

Ernie was to know such pride and happiness when he learned that Kate was pregnant. Fishing Cottage would be bursting at the seams but there was such joy, so many plans to be made that the future looked rosy for the new baby.

It was quite natural for babies to be born at home. Nursing homes were not for the likes of Kate.

The surgery at Twyford was not entirely happy with the position and conditions of Fishing Cottage. So to ensure the safe arrival of Kate's baby it was decided that as soon as the birth became imminent, she should move in with Ernie's parents at Hill Rise, Twyford. It was a usual occurrence for babies to be born at the home of one or other of the Grandparents and as Hill Rise was close to the doctor and district nurse, it was a sensible decision and one that met with the approval of both families.

The weather mid-October was mild with the morning mists blanketing the fields bordering the River Itchen, leaving St. Mary's Church rising up, as a maiden from the fog of memory of a long lost love.

Sunday dawned and with it, the realisation that the birth of Martin was soon to take place. The Drew household made their final preparations as the church bells rang out across the valley summoning the villagers to morning service. There was an authoritative air that echoed from the bell tower that few ignored. Ernie joined them for fear of doing anything to tempt fate lest it do other than smile upon his wife and first born.

The Sabbath would have been a quiet, restful and comparatively peaceful day on which to start on life's journey. But if the day of birth becomes the mould of the future, then Monday certainly shaped Martin's and ensured for all time a life of hard work, yet also bringing with it the compensation, the pleasurable side product of work well done, peace with yourself.

It was 19th October, 1925 and England was still very much a class conscious society. Domestic service was a prime source of employment as we see from

Harvey Nichols
of Knightsbridge

NEW COATS

FOR

WINTER WEAR

Moderate in price, exclusive in design, and made from best quality materials.

WELL-CUT COAT made from good quality ribbed velour and having a collar of natural fur, Racoon, Moleskin, Fox, or American Opossum. Lined throughout silk. In Black, Navy, Brown and other good colours.
PRICE
8½ Gns

SMART WALKING COAT made from new novelty ribbed velour, cut with the new godet flair, and trimmed on collar and flounce at sides with Opossum or Pulled Silver Coney fur. Lined throughout silk. In a few good colours.
PRICE **11½ Gns**

HANDSOME STREET COAT perfectly cut and tailored and made from good quality fine ribbed velour, collar, cuffs, and flounce trimmed Moleskin. Pulled Silver, Coney, or American Opossum fur. Lined throughout silk. In a few good colours. PRICE **17½ Gns**

HARVEY NICHOLS & CO., LTD., KNIGHTSBRIDGE, LONDON, S.W.1

The corner of Compton Street where Isaac and his family lived for a short time at Chequers (on the left hand side of the picture).

the columns of *The Times* newspaper, and the salaries shown are per year, averaging about £1 per week, London rates.

Fur trimming was much in evidence in women's fashion and fur coats still the envy of every young girl.

The social whirl of the middle and upper classes continued with Hunt and County Balls, still an important date on the social calendar.

Martin's world, however, continued at Fishing Cottage and the first event in his young life was his baptism at Compton Church, when he was just three weeks old. His Uncle Gordon was the proud Godfather and the Rev. Blackett, who had performed his parents' marriage ceremony, happily christened their son.

Around this time, Isaac was promoted to head dairyman and bore the promotion with both pride and the acceptance of one worthy of the task.

The family moved from Fishing Cottage to Chequers, which is on the corner of Compton Street. It was then a dairy.

Isaac planted the apple trees, mere saplings, but now the gnarled old trees that stand on the left-hand side of the front garden.

However, the stay at the Chequers was only for a short time.

ROUND THE SHOPS.

FASHIONS IN FUR COATS.

The fur trade is very busy just now and the departments in the drapery houses which cater for this class of business are experiencing a reaction in favour of the fur coat. The reason may be the fact that the fur-trimmed coat is almost a uniform, and though fur coats entail—if they are to be hard wearing—a considerable initial expenditure, they can be remodelled year after year. This year coats are so much shorter that a fur coat is not nearly so heavy to walk in as in former years. Consequently they can be worn oftener and by reason of their warmth they allow the very lightest frocks to be worn with them.

REVILLON FRÈRES, Regent-street, are showing fur coats of quality and beauty for the present season. There is a preference for brown furs this year and mink is the favourite with those who can afford what is really an investment. A Canadian mink coat will last for years and can be worn as either a day or evening wrap. Magnificent coats of this fur beautifully made from finely matched skins are being shown in new models. Moleskin coats and wraps, either in its natural shade or dyed bronze, blue, or green, with novel uses of the reverse working, show the tendency to flare more than other furs. Persian lamb, always a quiet and distinguished fur, is being trimmed this year with either kolinsky or mink, when made up into coats, the fashion being for a lighter fur to be used to trim a darker. In the same way one finds opossum dyed brown utilized to trim a fine coat of Hudson seal. Natural black musquash with the skins very cleverly worked to give the effect of width while keeping slim lines, makes a very handsome coat. Grey squirrel is a favourite fur this season and many handsome coats are made up with it. Leopardskin makes a notable coat for travelling or hard wear, and "susliki," a tawny grey fur, is being used for sports coats. Russian sable "choker" ties and long "scarf" wraps, beautiful fisher skins, and silver, cross, and blue fox of the finest quality are also being shown for present wear.

MARSHALL AND SNELGROVE, Oxford-street, have many novelties in umbrellas, some of which are in bright colours to match the new waterproofs. Many shades of green are popular for ordinary use, though brown is still strongly in favour. The short umbrella continues to sell, and the number of umbrellas purchased is really the result of the popularity of this style, which has become an interesting fashion accessory by reason of the many novel handles which are constantly introduced. Short crooks are finding a certain favour for use with tailored suits, while for dress wear lovely handles in dyed shagreen and ivory are useful for matching colours. Lapis-lazuli, amber, and goldstone are being used for handles of many kinds, and there is also a number of carved handles, mostly of birds in natural colourings, which are very pleasing. Among the novelties in bags are new pochettes, square in shape and decorated with real stones, such as onyx and cornelian.

HARRODS, Brompton-road, have just issued a booklet called "A Man's Occasions," covering the clothes needs of the well-dressed man. Their men's wear departments are a series of highly specialized little shops in each one of which there is a discriminating selection of the correct garment or accessory for every occasion. The booklet will be sent on request.

BURBERRYS, Haymarket, are holding from to-day until Friday winter sports parades with male and female mannequins. Their winter sports outfits are made from materials specially woven with smooth surfaces to which snow cannot cling and in bright colourings that show up well against the snow-covered backgrounds. The parades will take place from 11.30 to 1 p.m. and from 3 to 5 p.m. each day.

As Martin took his first faltering steps there was talk of council houses to be built on farm land just north of Compton Street. Kate and Ernie were later to learn that they were to be offered No. 19 (now re-numbered 18) and Isaac and Caroline were to be offered No. 21.

This was probably the highlight of their lives, a home of their own where Ernie would be Master and Kate able to exercise full responsibility for Martin. Not that the first two years of his life were without the lasting benefits often brought about by extremes. He had been surrounded by love but swinging from the indulgence of his parents to the tight rein of discipline held by Isaac. This brought about the unforgettable instances of awareness of the other side of the coin — that there are indeed two sides to everything. A lesson that stayed with him all his life and enabled him to see the other person's point of view. It moulded the gentle character of this lad for all time.

As Martin settled down into his new home he gradually soaked up the world around him like a voracious sponge. His heart was open and he became tuned into nature. For him a tree was music, a flower living poetry and the harvest sheer joy, a true thanksgiving. He watched the birds with increasing recognition and learned about trees and wild flowers. He scoured the skies for the sobbing storms that would soon lash the fields and he became steeped in country lore. He understood the signs that predicted sudden frosts or forthcoming drought. He belonged in the countryside, his spirit already entwined in nature; it was a symbiotic relationship and one so rare that it was almost sacred.

Time for school was approaching. The happiest days of his life? No, it was not so.

He had so much talent, a true aptitude for natural history, and an incredible ability for working with his hands. He possessed infinite patience and a strong artistic streak, all of which went unnoticed, untapped and unappreciated because he did not shine at the three R's. He was sorely undervalued.

This would not have happened under the ever watchful eye of today's Headmistress at Compton School. Dorothy Highfield ensures that every child is made aware of their own potential, to enable a measure of self-confidence to surface and she has a respect for all skills, academic and non-academic alike.

Surely this is the aim of all educationalists today. Sadly, it was not so in the 1930s. This resulted in Martin knowing complete and utter boredom. He concentrated on the school clock with more fervour than his studies, as the hands measured the day and were the authority on passing hours. As it ticked away, Martin regarded it with pleasure and studied it even more intently, lest a hand should happen to get held up along the way and a minute or two extra, in school, ensue. This clock, high on the wall of the big classroom, was to enter his life again at a later date.

The education of this small village school was considered satisfactory, as reported in the school log book. The same book gives an outline, a skeletal picture of school life during the 1930s.

The 1930s

The Compton School log book reports:

20.10.30
> Martin Drew admitted.

29.10.30
> One ton coal delivered.

30.10.30
> School closed for half term, two days.

21.11.30
> Average attendance 40.5. Low attendance due to two very wet days.

26.11.30
> Nurse called and examined children for signs of scarlet fever, as two cases reported.

28.11.30
> Average attendance 38.8. Low due to wet weather and outbreak of scarlet fever.

19.12.30
> Low attendance for week.

> School breaking up celebrations took place in afternoon. Christmas Holidays two weeks until January 5th, 1931.

26.01.31
> 15½ cwt coal delivered.

18.02.31
> Children in church — Ash Wednesday.

05.03.31
> Closed school at 3.20 and forfeited play in order to perform Festival of Music at concert in the parish hall.

01.04.31
> School closed for Easter Holiday.

14.04.31
> School re-assembled.

14.05.31
> Ascension Day. School closed in afternoon.

Compton Rectory garden where the church fete was held. The building is now St. Patrick's and was formerly the Red House.

22.05.31

Empire Day celebrated in morning in playground from 11 onwards. School closed in afternoon for Empire Day and for one week WHITSUN.

01.06.31

School re-opened.

01.07.31

Holiday in afternoon for children to attend church fete in Rectory garden.

24.07.31

One ton coal.

28.07.31

One ton coke.

29.07.31

Half ton coke.

31.07.31

School closed for August holiday. One month.

31.08.31

School re-opened.

07.09.31

Mr. Jupe came from the office and brought 14 dual desks and removed old long desks from upper room.

09.09.31

Six choir boys left school during afternoon to attend wedding.

18.09.31

Five cwt of peat arrived. Canon P. Cunningham sometimes checked registers.

29.09.31

Report from H.M.I. arrived — Mr. K. J. Ritchie.

This small school continues to do well. The demeanour of children is excellent and there is every sign of careful and systematic teaching in both classes. The general level of work in fundamental subjects is thoroughly sound except for a falling off in arithmetic at the top. Spelling is exceptionally good throughout. The answers to written questions given to older children and oral questions given to stds. IV and V on history and geography showed only a moderate knowledge but fair to point out children only back a week after summer holidays. Handwork well above average quality. As to singing it may be mentioned that in this year's Winchester Festival, this school, the smallest competing, gained third place in aggregate marks. Building, playground well and carefully looked after. Suggested that lighting in infant room would be improved by the lopping of adjacent trees.

22.10.31

School closed half term (Friday and Monday) and Election Day Tuesday 27th as school used as Polling Station.

Rector took scriptures each week.

Miss Northover   Teacher

14.12.31

School closed in afternoon for children to attend dress rehearsal for Christmas play at Parish Hall.

18.12.31

'Breaking Up' festivity visit of Father Christmas. School closed two weeks.

11.02.32 to 16.02.32

Half term.

23.03.32 to 05.04.32

Easter.

24.05.32

Closed afternoon. Empire Day.

21.06.32

Mr. A. Joliffe visited and lectured on Alcohol and the Brain.

28.07.32

Headmistress resigns her charge of this school today. Successful in interviews at New Milton regarding Wootton School.

Temporary Headmistress 29.08.32 to 30.09.32.

03.10.32

Dorothy Emily Francis White started as Headmistress.

07.11.32

Afternoon session commenced 1 p.m. and will continue so during Nov., Dec., Jan. and Feb. Closing at 3.30.

11.11.32

Two minutes' silence observed.

12.12.32

Father Christmas visited and distributed presents.

05.05.33

Chicken pox also scarlet fever.

07.06.33

Closed. Elder children taken to Aldershot tattoo.

12.06.33

49 children on roll.

12.07.33

Closed for annual summer outing.

29.07.33

Michaelmas Day — Service in church.

02.02.34

Conjuror visited and entertained during dinner hour.

12.03.34

Choir of 17 children entered for Winchester and County Music Festival, obtaining second place and gaining a banner and certificate.

School outing – Martin (in blazer) and his friend, Peter (far right) on the beach at Brighton.

16.04.34

Scarlet fever. One child reported to medical officer. Nurse examined other children.

29.11.34

Holiday by command of His Majesty the King on occasion of the marriage of the Duke of Kent and Princess Marina.

25.03.35

Saturday 23rd, a choir of 17 children taken to Winchester to take part in County Festival competition for children's choirs of smaller elementary schools, third place out of 14 choirs.

29.03.35

Last day of school year. (It is interesting to note the end of school year was in March instead of July as we have it.)

01.04.35

First day of new school year.

06.05.35

Holiday for King's Silver Jubilee.

10.05.35

No afternoon session. 32 children taken to see the films of the King's reign, Royal Cavalcade and Jubilee procession.

24.04.35

Empire Day. Children marched past and saluted the flag and sang the national anthem.

06.11.35

Holiday because of the marriage of H.R.H. Duke of Gloucester.

14.11.35

Closed. Polling Station General Election.

28.01.36

Closed funeral King George V.

25.05.36

With permission of Managers, stds. VII and VI 17 children to go to railway at water meadows Shawford to watch train carrying Royal Family to Southampton, go by.

16.07.36

Listened to broadcast of King presenting new colours to Battalion of Guard.

23.07.36

No school. Hospital fete.

30.09.36

Approval received to alteration of timetable to include broadcast lessons during autumn term. Broadcasts such as 'Finding very old homes', 'How to read nature's story books', 'Roman homes in Britain', 'How the plough changed Britain', 'North Island, New Zealand', 'How our habits make our homes', 'Rats and Voles', 'Birds that flock together', 'The earliest English homes', 'Spring flowers', 'Roads', 'Evergreens'.

11.11.36

Listened to service of Remembrance from Cenotaph.

01.12.36

Sale of children's needlework and knitting took place during afternoon.

13.04.37

Chair for Headteacher's desk delivered.

15.03.39

Mrs. Longhurst, an A.R.P. warden for Compton, came into school at 10 a.m. to see that gas masks were properly adjusted.

27.06.39

Closed for summer outing to Bognor.

20.07.39

Mrs. Longhurst, A.R.P. warden, came to test and try respirators.

20.09.39

School re-opened after 6½ weeks, five weeks' summer holiday and 1½ weeks compulsory closing under the Board of Education Emergency Scheme.

Admitted six privately evacuated children.

Twelve Government evacuated children from Portsmouth.

05.10.39

Hours changed 1.30 to 3.45.

21.12.39

Breaking up. Father Christmas left toys and sweets. Martin Drew left, age exempt.

Compton village, its church and school were about to enter the war years and although not devastated by world events, their lives were to be touched and changed forever. Village life was to open up as the outside world came bursting into their living rooms through the wireless that, by now, most homes owned.

Before looking into the years of the war, let us first read between the lines of the school log book that spans Martin's school days.

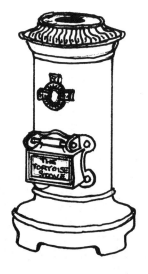

Planting a seed

Martin reached his fifth birthday in the knowledge that the following day his school life would begin and this held no great joy. For even at this young age he loved to be outside, to potter about the garden mirroring his father's actions.

Mrs. Burn, wife of the churchwarden, recalls watching him carry a green vase to her garden and fill it with soil using a dessert spoon he had carried from home. When she asked what he was doing, he replied "planting a seed for my mummy" and he put his chubby hand in his trouser pocket and brought out some seeds. Sixty years on and now living at Brendon Care Nursing Home she remembers the incident as if it were yesterday and says "I've always wondered whether it grew".

Compton school had two classrooms called simply the big room and the little room. The heating was by coal and coke. The big room had a tortoise stove and its voracious appetite was appeased by the constant shovelling on of coke, by the teachers themselves; although the skuttles were filled from the bunker early in the morning by the caretaker, Fred Roberts, who, incidentally, lived next door to Martin and was the means by which news of Martin's misdoings reached his parents quicker than normal bush telegraph.

The little room had a coal fire which was both amiable and controllable.

The tortoise stove was often at the mercy of the elements and when the wind blew in the wrong direction, the room filled with smoke so that it was impossible to see across the classroom. The doors were then opened to let out the smoke, along with all the heat.

Martin's memories were of being very cold, at school, during the winters. For to sit close to the stove was also to sit close to the teacher and this he avoided as it was easier to drift through the day from a distance.

The big room had a beautiful large arched window. Outside the room, facing the churchyard was a covered shelter made of corrugated iron on square posts. It was open all the way round but nevertheless afforded some shelter in bad weather and the children were allowed to play there.

It was under this shelter, every Friday, that the older boys prepared the ink wells for the following week's work. They collected up the porcelain pots and soon learned that by putting a little blotting paper at the bottom before filling with ink, the recipient would produce some messy work decorated with ink blots, on Monday morning. It seems that any girl currently out of favour with the lads would find herself on the receiving end, especially as the boys found this an irksome task and began to resent the fact that this chore was not carried out on a rota basis.

Martin with friends during harvesting.

One day, throwing caution to the wind along with the ink wells, they gave vent to their frustration, and then watched in horror as the pots landed in the churchyard, splashing ink onto some of the gravestones.

As well as receiving several strokes of the cane, their punishment was not complete until many hours had been spent scrubbing the graves.

A great delight to Martin was the small school garden, which the older boys tended, leaving the girls in school with their needlework. Society was still very much divided into the male and female role, and this was a subtle preparation for the life that would confront them, beyond the confines of the school walls.

However, Martin loved these days and was at home with the tools. This was not the case with one youngster who used a garden hoe as a weapon, following an argument with another lad. They all watched in horror as the blond curls of this frightened boy became red with blood and he was taken off, for the wound to be stitched.

The culprit was severely punished and nobody had any quarrel with that decision. In addition, gardening was stopped for a long time causing Martin and his friends to feel much aggrieved. In fact, it was the beginning of the end of school gardening, for when war broke out in 1939 an underground Anderson air raid shelter was to occupy their gardening patch.

The children spent many hours sitting underground during the years of the war, as the teachers took them down as soon as the air raid sirens sounded.

The school had a croquet set which the children used at play times. One day, a few of the older boys managed to hold a school mate on the ground by sitting on him while others put the croquet hoop round his neck and pushed the ends into the ground just before they were called in from play. They ran in, as the teacher became increasingly irritated by the seemingly defiant behaviour of the boy on the ground. She shouted for him to 'come at once' before marching over to the prostrate figure.

Martin and his friends were absolutely delighted at the success of their joke and felt the day was really turning out to be quite a promising one.

If ever a joke misfired, that one did and Martin and his friends were taken in front of the whole school and caned, as well as being severely lectured on the possible dangers.

Martin always enjoyed the handwork lessons when the boys made rugs. Plain canvas was used and the children made their own patterns, cutting the wool themselves from large hanks.

In order to hold the canvas in place, they opened their desks and wedged the canvas in the slit where the lid was hinged. On closing the desk, the canvas was secured for working. Martin was considered the best at rug making and his were taken home by the teacher.

There were never any lack of volunteers for the church choir and as long as they produced a reasonable sound, they were accepted. Martin joined at the earliest possible opportunity when he realised that the choir boys were allowed to leave school whenever they were needed for church services. They walked through the gate near their classroom, into the churchyard and the glorious freedom from the schoolroom.

The school play area was small as the present car park gate was then a five-bar wooden gate into the farmer's field. The cows would look over the fence at the children reminding them that this was indeed a country school.

Cricket was popular with the boys and they played in the field next to Cherrycroft. The actual pitch was in line with Church Lane (Carmens Lane). This was another playtime activity that remained unsupervised, although there is no record of any mishap.

Martin endured rather than enjoyed his schooldays. Life was grey and blurred but outside the restrictions of the school room, the world was in sharp focus and full of colour. As a country lad, he knew the joy and comfort that enveloped body and soul as he walked homeward through the village and watched the smoke curling up into the evening sky, from the neighbouring chimneys, signalling a fire in the hearth to thaw his frozen fingers.

The river at Shawford. Above: The Locks.

The Cat Steps on Compton Down where Martin played as a young boy and where, sadly, his father died.

The warmth of the wood fires brought such comfort to farmers and gardeners alike, as they returned home, weary and cold after a day battling with the elements. They used dry beech twigs for kindling and then sat in the well-worn comfortable armchairs, stoking the fire as the flames licked the logs.

Martin's father collected and stored logs enough to see his family through the cold winter days. He loved to get hold of apple, pear, plum or cherry as they filled the room with such a pleasant scent, but he was happy to cut and store any wood as insurance against the winter chill.

Fishing was another popular holiday past-time and the children would set off for Shawford river, their spirits rising with the fish, a jam sandwich in their pockets to ward off the pangs of hunger, a natural by-product of fresh air and excitement.

Martin and his friend, Pete, caught minnows by tying string round the neck of jam jars and lowering them into the river which would be brimming after a rainfall. A net was a luxury they couldn't claim; nevertheless the fun could not have been surpassed had they possessed the most elaborate of equipment.

This same river, winding its way through the water meadows, was also the scene of their swimming, with the youngsters diving off the locks. They felt the river could be trusted, it was not as reckless as the sea. The gentle countryside had tamed this relative of the raging roaring ocean.

When they tired of their water sports, they returned to the fields and made dens in the hangers opposite the cat steps. The cat steps on Compton Down were so named because the steps resembled large cat prints on the hillside.

They used branches from the nearby trees and spent hours in their dens. At Judd's farm copse, they collected primroses and bluebells to present to their mothers, knowing it would soothe and soften the sharp words which might otherwise follow the muddy knees and scuffed shoes as they arrived late for their tea. Time had little meaning to the children of the village during school holidays. Not that, by any means, it was all play. It was certainly all enjoyment for the work itself was such enormous pleasure to Martin.

From a very tender age, he worked in the fields. Child labour on the farm was invaluable, especially during haymaking and harvest. These children had a natural feel for the seasons and were able to pair the work to the time of year.

Martin never lost this way of working, of taking his time. Nature can not be hurried and Martin quickly learned the wisdom of this fact, both on the farms and the gardens where his father worked. He absorbed and respected the quirks of nature.

Although only a young man, Ernie's long back had the beginnings of a curve that was to become impossible to straighten later on. A legacy with which many gardeners will readily identify.

As the days of winter faded into memory, Martin would watch the catkins gradually turning golden brown. He would look up at the two elm trees that stood tall and proud in the corner where the school pond is now sited. It was well known by country folk that elm trees are safe if the rooks nest in them as it was never known for a rookery to be found in a diseased or rotten elm tree.

He knew where to find aconites and white violets and loved the sticky chestnut buds.

There was great excitement when threshing time arrived. Martin was completely mesmerised by the rally of steam engines (reminiscent of a fair) that passed through the village, followed by the threshing machine. It toured the countryside with every farmer eagerly awaiting his turn for the ricks to be threshed.

This is where the youngsters earned a few pennies as, armed with sticks, they chased and killed the rats. Martin worked hard, knowing the farmer would pay a penny (1d) per tail (today's equivalent would be ½p).

The farmer threw the rats onto a heap and Martin, on at least one occasion, walked to the back of the heap and retrieved a rat for presenting a second time and for a second penny.

The biggest change in farming in the area was the arrival of the combine harvester which cut and threshed the corn, leaving neatly tied up sacks in the field; although Martin missed the countryside beauty of the stooks and ricks, bearing witness to the labour of harvest, to the healthy sweat wrung from hours of toil.

Once the crop had been gathered and stored away, an air of satisfaction hung over the valley equal to an old man sitting on his porch on a summer's evening and puffing on his pipe as he remembered the hard days that had become but a distant memory.

Martin had his first smoke when he discovered peth bind (clematis) could be used. This was cut and dried until hard. Martin and Pete sat up in their den on Compton Down and lit the makeshift cigarettes. Their eyes watered and they choked as they drifted for a while into the world of adults. Sometimes Martin would collect the ends of his father's cigarettes and fill the peth bind with the spent tobacco. How many more youngsters started a lifetime's smoking habit through something as innocent and beautiful as clematis, the lovely 'old man's beard' that trailed over the hedges like a veil gently caressing the head of a young bride?

Rabbits were staple diet for the families, and when cooked in large earthenware pots with garden vegetables, filled many an empty tummy. The children, as young as eight years, went out into the fields with sticks to catch the rabbits which, of course, were real pests in the world of farming.

There were so many superstitions and folklore woven into countryside living and Martin absorbed them all. Midsummer day was a forecast guide, for if it should rain then, nuts would be scarce. Should the day be bathed in sunshine a good corn harvest was ensured.

'A wet May, plenty of hay' and that would mean all the boys helping in the fields turning the hay for drying and building the hayricks — which were an art in themselves and as beautiful as any painting, poem or concerto.

June was a favourite month of Martin's. The days were warm and the long balmy evenings stretched their leisure time.

It was a month of noticeable fragrance and none more potent than that of the Spanish chestnuts. From the creamy feathery blossom, the wind would carry the heady scent along the country lanes. Martin was to meet this unforgettable tree further along his life's path.

In the fields, Martin helped with hand weeding midst the corn, using a forked stick. The thistles were never cut before St. John's Day (24th June)

47

'The hangars' where Martin and his friends had their den and where Martin first started smoking. To the boys it resembled an airfield hangar – in their imagination.

because as an old verse, known to all countryman and religiously adhered to by Martin's father, told them:

> *"Thistles cut in May*
> *Come up again next day*
> *Thistles cut in June*
> *Come up again soon*
> *Cut them in July*
> *They'll be sure to die."*

The days slowly headed towards harvest and the fields were silent as the sunlight streamed down upon the earth. The cornfields came into their own as the ripening process neared completion. The patches of scarlet poppies decorated the golden red crops. The countryside was full and ripe and the woodland paths embroidered with a profusion of wild flowers, purple vetch, agrimony, hawkweed, speedwells and pimpernels.

Martin loved the humble scarlet pimpernel and noted that it closed its petals against forthcoming rain, earning itself the reputation of being the poor man's weather-glass but it served Martin well until many years later he was to receive a more reliable weather guide.

As summer began to give way to autumn, Martin would walk over Shawford Downs for his own private illumination display which he has always insisted, rivalled Blackpool's any time!

The chalk downs were switched on by hundreds of glow-worms so that the hillside was dotted with bright green lights. Martin would sometimes carry a few home and put them on his lawn; they never stayed very long.

When autumn days had faded, winter preparations began. As the trees shed their leaves and stood tall and naked against the sky-line, the folk in the village ferreted around in cupboards and drawers for their winter woollies, their tried and trusted insurance against the forthcoming frosts and chilly winds.

Their outer bodies taken care of, it was left to the ever simmering stewpot to warm from within. This produced a thick rich gravy into which chunks of bread were dipped. How Martin enjoyed this and throughout his life relished bread dipping into rich stews and gravies! Another culinary delight was pheasant but none tasted more satisfying than those occasionally and craftily poached, by his father, as a welcome treat for their palates, following a surfeit of rabbit.

As the eve of All Saints' Day approached Martin would carve a face in a pumpkin and light up the mystic features with a small candle.

There were few celebrations in his life as the years were marked by the seasons, rather than by outside artificial events so Martin made the most of them culminating in the celebration of Christmas. It was such a special event for him. The one occasion when all good things came his way. Food in plenty and time to enjoy it, the hands of the clock stilled against passing hours. Families together in their own homes; a fire crackling away in the hearth and the log basket filled with cherry and apple wood with a collection of fir cones.

Martin would collect holly and decorate all pictures and photographs. The high mantlepiece adorned with small pieces of holly entwined with ivy, was a sure tribute to the dormant artistry within this lad.

When he was older, he cut a slit in the bark of one of his father's apple trees before rubbing in some mistletoe berries. This, in due course, produced fine Christmas decoration which still grows in the apple tree in Attwoods Drove, today.

Martin never lost this childlike wonder of Christmas, the carols, churchbells, cakes and puddings heavy with fruit, mulled wine and days naked of pretence, when sheer joy and happiness could surface and even shine. No school and later no work either on these special days. Love and contentment flourished and cemented the magical moments in his heart for all time. The spell was cast.

There is only ever one quiet place for all of us and it is within ourselves. It was finally in having time to shut out the world and its work that Martin found the peace of Christmas.

As the embers of the old year slowly cooled and died, the folk of Compton regularly braced themselves for the arrival of January and February whilst acknowledging the necessary and vital role these babes of the New Year played, they were only truly appreciated when they had grown to March and April and life was, once again, beginning to stir. The initial stirring was often from beneath a covering of snow. Farmers and gardeners, alike, realised it was all part of their yearly cycle of survival.

By watching the birds, it was known when snow was on the way, as they came flocking to the woods for shelter and as the icy winds roared up the valley, Martin prepared to watch for the telltale tracks that would soon be seen on the white blanket covering the countryside.

Birds, pheasants, rabbits and foxes could all be traced and so, too, could Martin, by his welly boot tracks!

For better or worse this hard, but idyllic lifestyle was nearing its end. The war was gradually becoming grim reality, and homes all over the country were having their lives changed for ever.

Christmas, 1939 was a sombre affair, compared with Christmases past.

Compton School, as yet, relatively untouched by the world conflict, arranged the usual annual visit of Father Christmas. He arrived on 21st December bringing toys and sweets for all the children before they broke up for the holiday.

This was Martin's last Christmas as a schoolchild. He was only just 14 years old and was about to enter the great British Work Force. His world was expanding and life would soon take him from the village in the valley, to the City of Winchester, beyond.

The reins that had guided his progress at school, were held by 'Govvy' White (Governess White, as she was called by parents). They had been held with authority and great kindness but with little imagination. Had the reins been relaxed or even released awhile and Martin given his head just long enough to see which path he would travel, the latent abilities of this quiet country lad might have been given firm foundations on which to grow and flourish. If only his undoubtable talents had been recognised and nurtured, instead of supressed as he was protestingly but surely squeezed into a mould he did not and could not fit, he would probably have come to love his village school and consequently taken his leave of it with some sadness instead of with the euphoria that accompanied his going.

However, the teaching he had received stood him in good stead as he set off to join the staff at Hillier and Sons, the local nursery gardeners.

Shop of E. Hillier, Nurseryman,
Seedsman and Florist, 95 High Street, c.1895

The arrival of this day saw the culmination of Kate and Ernie's dreams, hopes and prayers. They could be forgiven their smug smiles. Not for their son, the uncertain future that walked hand in hand with Ernie's work as a jobbing gardener. Not for Martin the misery of reduced wages at the end of a week when perhaps the Admiral didn't want him on the usual Monday because it was Christmas Day or maybe the Colonel told him not to come that week because it had been snowing and he had already cleared his paths or the Lady he worked for every Wednesday was giving a garden party and didn't want Ernie hovering. These enforced holidays were unpaid, unavoidable and very unhappy as Kate struggled to make ends meet.

There was one occasion when his employer had no change in the house and with "I'll pay you next week, Drew", ringing in his ears, Ernie was left to wonder whether he, in turn, could pass this same statement to the rent man!

Martin cycled to West Hill Nursery (now called Winchester Garden Centre). His first job every morning was to clean the shoes of the Hillier family (then living at Pinaster, the house next to Winchester Prison).

One of his earliest recollections was of being asked by Mr. Edwin Hillier to bring a cyclamen plant from the greenhouse to Pinaster, as decoration for a party that evening.

Martin chose carefully and presented a perfect specimen — only to be told "That one's too good, boy. Take it back. I can sell that in the shop"!

One year later, and still only 15 years old Martin moved to the St. Cross Nursery where he was to spend the next 20 years and where, incidentally, Martin met Margaret, his future wife, and they were married in May 1956. This was the only Chelsea Show year that Martin missed. Consequently, he and his wife never spent one of their next 33 wedding anniversaries together (more about the 34th later).

St. Cross Nursery specialised in alpines, herbaceous and water plants. They also did a brisk trade in water snails, packing them up and sending them by post.

When it became obvious that the war was more than a passing problem and that every man, woman and child would be called upon to play a part, the world of horticulture had to take stock of its direction and decorative plants gave way to fruit and vegetables.

In the war effort, Hillier's played their part to the full and in so doing developed techniques which were to stand them in good stead in future years.

The Air Ministry requested them to develop ways of lifting and transplanting large trees to camouflage aircraft hangars. In order to do this it was necessary that they should be 30ft. to 50ft. in height.

This was successfully accomplished as well as 'portable' hedgerows that could be wheeled into place for instant disguise of military installations.

As Martin cycled towards the nursery, on a warm sunny day in 1940, he found it impossible to believe that war could ever come to such a day, but all the beautiful days of the next few summers were to be tainted by world events and Compton village was to suffer some of the pain.

An incendiary bomb was dropped on the village, causing great consternation. Everyone was out in their best clothes trying to put out the fire — and the second bomb that narrowly missed the church brought undisguised anger, 'How dare they!'.

Its mark can still be seen on the tombstone by the boiler house steps at the side of the church.

When a plane came down at Twyford, there was a rush across the downs to take a look. Martin, who was already interested in aircraft, remembered every detail.

The boys started collecting the shrapnel that was scattered all over the village and as their collections grew, so, too, did the realisation that this was not a game but something history would record, with distaste.

There were lighter moments, such as the time when an obnoxious smell hovered over the village. Mrs. Longhurst, who had undertaken gas mask control, ran around everywhere instructing folk to put on their gas masks, only to find out later that the offence was not German orientated but due to the local farmer and silage!

Compton was soon to learn that this was also a children's war, as schoolchildren from Portsmouth were evacuated to the relative safety of the countryside. The evacuation started as Britain declared war on Germany and bomb attacks were feared on the cities. Evacuation day proved to be premature and soon parents wanted their children home again as the phoney war took over. Many evacuees left Compton and its school, only to return hurriedly after Portsmouth had been savagely blitzed.

Parents suffered continual conflict as their desire to have their children home was weighed against their wish for their youngsters' safety; whilst acknowledging the possibility of a lonely survival for their offspring should they, themselves, perish in war-torn Portsmouth. Most of them tucked this thought away and, with it, the realisation that many adults would, indeed, be sacrificed if the children were to have a future.

For one Portsmouth family, such a future was not ensured. Little Roger Harris was evacuated to Compton and joined in the life of the village school where he was much loved. He was taken ill in January, 1942 and died in Winchester Hospital. His family decided that he should remain in Compton.

On the grave of Roger, the inscription read: 'In loving memory of our dear little son Roger Harris who passed away 20 Jan. 1942 aged nine years. Also his beloved brother, Bob, presumed killed on H.M.S. Hood – *24 May 1941.'*

He was buried beneath a tree in Compton Churchyard, within sight of the school and his playmates.

This poor family were to know more sadness, as their elder son, a young sailor, was drowned at sea when his ship (H.M.S. *Hood*) was sunk. They were deprived the comfort of a Christian burial and so decided to have his name added to Roger's, thereby ensuring their two sons would be together, if only in names on a gravestone at Compton.

The school log book tells of the war years as Martin continued his daily work at Hillier's nursery.

The War — as recorded
by Compton School

20.9.39

School re-opened this morning at 9 o'clock, after 6½ weeks, five weeks summer holiday and 1½ weeks compulsory closing under the Board of Education Emergency Scheme. One resident child admitted.

Six privately evacuated children.

Sixteen Government evacuated children, from Portsmouth.

25.9.39

Two extra Government evacuated children on the roll.

2.10.39

Two evacuated children have gone back to Portsmouth.

16.1.40

The new Rector of the parish, Rev. E. E. S. Utterton, came and took a scripture lesson with the elder children.

24.5.40

Empire Day, a talk on origin and meaning was given. The Rector came in and took some prayers for Empire Day. Two Empire hymns were sung and the National Anthem. The sum of one guinea was collected to be sent to the overseas league, to provide tobacco and cigarettes for the Troops; each child who subscribed was given a coloured overseas souvenir card.

Broadcast Talk. A short talk on the Empire by representatives from Canada, Zululand and Australia.

8.7.40

One child died under an operation during the weekend.

One child admitted for the duration of the war.

11.7.40

All the children brought flowers from their own gardens to put on the grave of their little friend. The elder ones attended the service in church and sang two hymns.

24.9.40

The Winchester siren sounded at five minutes to 11 a.m., the 'all clear' at 11.20. The children went to the shelter.

21.10.40

One privately evacuated child from London admitted.

24.10.40

One Government evacuated child from London admitted.

4.11.40

Four evacuated children admitted. One from Portsmouth, three from London (Government).

7.11.40

The Winchester siren sounded at 2.30. The children went to the shelter. The 'all clear' went at 3.15.

29.1.41

Dr. Marsden Roberts attended this afternoon at 2.15 and inoculated 30 children against diphtheria.

18.2.41

One can of Izal, two battery lanterns and one nozzle for stirrup pump have been received for shelter of the school.

19.2.41

A load of sand for sandbags has been delivered.

20.2.41

Six sandbags have been delivered. They have been half-filled with sand and placed at the doors of the school.

20.3.41

School closed this afternoon for a confirmation service.

12.8.41

The Infant class went to the end of the village at 10 a.m. to see the corn cut in one of the fields.

20.10.41

Seventeen children helped on three farms with potato picking during the holiday.

26.1.42

Roger Harris a Portsmouth evacuated child attending this school, died of pneumonia last week in Winchester Hospital, to the great sorrow of all at school, he was very much loved.

20.2.42

This morning 63 blankets and three camp beds were delivered at the school.

23.2.42

Mr. Worboys, the Portsmouth evacuated Master, finished work in this school this afternoon, having been recalled to Portsmouth to start again after the Easter holiday. School closed this afternoon for Good Friday and Easter Monday.

26.6.42

The black-out frames and curtains for the school windows to be used in the event of it being required for a rest centre, were finished and fitted this week.

26.10.42

Winchester and Otterbourne sirens sounded, children went to shelter from 11.40 to 12 o'clock. Much gun fire. Sirens sounded, dinner children went to shelter from 12.35 to 12.55.

27.10.42

Winchester sirens sounded at 1.20 p.m., children waited in playground by shelter until 1.40.

28.10.42

Sirens sounded at 8.40 a.m. Children waited until 9.05 a.m.

5.11.42

Sirens sounded at 10.20 a.m., children were dressed ready for shelter. 'All clear' sounded at 10.50.

30.11.42

Winchester sirens sounded, children went to shelter from 11 a.m. to 11.30 a.m.

12.2.43

Winchester sirens sounded at 10 minutes to 12 this morning. Children went to shelter. 'All clear' sounded at 12.10 p.m.

16.2.43

Winchester siren sounded this morning. Children went to shelter for a short time.

4.3.43

Five evacuated children from Hursley admitted, having moved to a Hostel (Government) in Compton.

5.3.43

Two evacuated children admitted temporarily from Hostel in Compton.

24.5.43

Empire Day. A service was held in the church at 11 a.m. for children, parents and friends, followed by an Empire address by Lady Burstall. The address was given in the church as the weather was so wet.

The flag was afterwards saluted in school.

29.6.43

An evacuated child (Government) admitted for one month (billeted at Greystones Hostel).

2.7.43

Winchester sirens sounded at 2.55 p.m., children went to shelter. 'All clear' went at 3.15 p.m.

6.8.43

School was closed for this afternoon with permission of County Education Officer, so that furniture and floor of Infant room could be washed with disinfectant, a child who was sick in the room during the week has since been taken to the isolation hospital with scarlet fever.

11.10.43

School re-opened. Canteen dinners commenced, 41 children stayed to dinner.

Rev. Utterton and Mr. Fearon called. No fires on account of there being no kindling wood. Caretaker refused to use brushwood.

14.10.43

Mr. Fearon called about stove in large classroom which fills the room with smoke thus necessitating frequent absences from the room, by the children, to obtain fresh air.

19.10.43

Rev. Utterton took seniors for scripture. Mr. Newman removed a dead rook from the stove pipe in the large classroom thus removing the cause of the smoke we have endured.

21.4.44

£29 was brought in war savings for 'Salute the Soldier' week.

20.10.44

About 20 children from the upper department were taken out during the last lesson on two afternoons to gather hips.

13.2.45

A Police Officer and Lieutenant of the East Lancashires visited and gave a talk on the dangers of picking up stray bombs or metal of any kind.

8.5.45

School closed for two days for VE-Day.

Children began leaving Compton School to return to Portsmouth.

5.7.45

No school, premises being used as a Polling Station.

The war was over leaving Britain battered but not bowed.

Peace . . .

Compton slowly came to life as black-out curtains and shutters were removed from windows, allowing the glow from the cottages to light the way homeward, once more.

Many prayers of thanksgiving were said in Compton Church for, indeed, Compton had much for which to give thanks.

When the Rev. Edmund William Morley died at Compton on March 13th, 1946, his wife presented the church with a little figure on the crucifix above the pulpit.

It has a strange history. It was picked up 'somewhere in France' in 1916 by the Rev. Morley, who was serving with the Red Cross. It was amongst the rubble of a church in a devastated area. As he was unable to return it to the unknown church he took care of it until the war was over; when it was placed on a cross of oak.

Martin joined the confirmation class at the beginning of 1945 and was confirmed by the Bishop of Southampton, who travelled to Compton for the ceremony. Martin's first communion was on Mothering Sunday (11th March).

Meanwhile, he continued learning all that he could about the plants he handled and each year as Christmas neared, he left the nursery in order to make holly wreaths at Hillier's shop in Winchester High Street and then later at West Hill Nursery.

He was adept at twisting the prickly twigs of Christmas into beautiful tributes to grace many churchyards during the yule-tide season.

When St. Cross Nursery was sold for building, Martin moved to Ampfield House to work in the walled garden from where he moved to Broadgate Farm until the Show Department came to rest at the Container Unit.

Whilst at Broadgate Farm he noticed a Russell Lupin seedling in one of the stock beds that was unlike any other he had seen. It was a beautiful clear yellow that reminded him of a summer's day. He asked Roy Lancaster (plantsman, writer and broadcaster who was, at that time, working at Hillier's) to look at it and he confirmed that it was indeed new to the nursery trade. A new plant, Martin was thrilled and this lovely Lupin was named 'Broadgate Yellow'.

It was so typical of Martin, this awareness of plants and of all living things. In his quiet, gentle way he absorbed it all. It was unnecessary to consciously look, for he sensed the changes taking place. He recognised the differences, knew the expected flowering times and at what stage, the trees would once

Above Compton Church pulpit is the 'little figure' that was picked up 'somewhere in France' during the First World War.

again show their mantle of green. And how he looked forward to this. He fervently welcomed the new growth that signalled the end of winter and was so happy to bid farewell to the cold unfriendly months of the year. Never more so than in 1958 for it was during the winter that a tree blew down in a storm and it fell across the cat steps on the nearby Downs. Martin's father, Ernie, asked the farmer if he could have it as he knew it would provide logs to stoke his fire for many months.

He set off with his axe but never returned. It was Martin's sad task, on looking for his father, to find him dead. He was just 59 years old. It had been one tree too many, for this hard working man.

Martin and Margaret Drew on their wedding day, 19th May, 1956.

Martin (left) with workmate John Knight enjoying a lunch break in the packing shed at Hillier's Nursery.

International success —
and his school clock!

Martin continued working with herbaceous plants until the late 1960s, travelling thousands of miles exhibiting at all the major shows and winning top awards.

By now, he and his wife had settled down in Martin's Fields, Compton and his daughters, Elaine and Sarah, were themselves attending the village school. At this same school his wife worked as a dinner lady before combining it with the more arduous task of caretaker.

Martin helped in the school whenever he was home and it was at this point that the old school clock entered his life once more. Climbing up to clean the top of a large tall cupboard, Margaret discovered a dirty, dusty looking box which Martin recognised instantly. Quickly wiping away the cobwebs, he discovered the old time-piece of his school days. He was overjoyed and glancing at the battered face and bent hands of the familiar old friend he had once watched so intently, asked permission to take it home to repair. Martin loved clocks — the 'proper' ones as he called them. He had no interest in any operated by either battery or electricity.

His infinite patience, once again, came to the fore and his large hands with strong fingers were as nimble as those of any surgeon, as he handled the smallest cog on the tiniest wheel. He spent many happy hours repairing clocks and watches for friends, so the Compton school clock was in very safe hands. After many hours of work it was returned to school where it now ticks away, marking the hours with the appropriate number of strikes.

It was in 1970 that Martin was given overall responsibility by Hillier's for the shows and he exhibited trees, shrubs and perennials, working long hours to make sure he produced the best possible result. He refused to settle for less than perfection.

Opposite top: From left to right, Elaine Drew, Geoffrey Elliott, Jimmy Collins, Ann Montgomery.
Below: Starting far left - by blackboard and coming up left hand side across near top and down right hand side: Sarah Drew, Linda Edwards, Sarah Arnold, Irene Hargood, Sara Greasly (one elbow on desk, her left arm up to face), Jonathan Lincoln, Ben Le Bas, Katrina Johnston, Caroline Sweetman (short curly hair looking at camera), Melody Lawrence, Christopher Brett (far right by door).

The old school clock.

Sir Harold Hillier was eager to obtain the Rothschild Challenge Cup for Rhododendrons as it was one of the few trophies eluding Hillier's.

Martin was delighted when, finally, in 1973, he was able to bring it home and, for good measure, won it again in 1976.

This same year he went to Italy, with Robert Hillier, accompanied by Lady Hillier, where they won several awards at the International Show at Genoa.

This was Martin's first, and only, time abroad and how he soaked up the experience!

Success followed success as he travelled the countryside and sandwiched between the shows were displays at large stores such as Debenhams at Southampton and Selfridges and Harrods in London as well as finding time for many decorating jobs, everything from ploughing matches to Cathedrals.

Martin, receiving congratulations from Lady Hillier, John and Robert Hillier.

Honoured

It was on 15th October, 1977 that Martin received a letter from the Royal Horticultural Society, telling him that the President and Council proposed electing him as an Associate of Honour and asking if it would be agreeable to him. Would it? Martin was delighted and honoured and so happy.

He was asked that the matter be kept confidential, until the annual awards were published in the press, early in December.

This gave Martin no trouble at all. It was enough to have been proposed. *He* knew. That the world, in general, was ignorant of the fact, took nothing from the tremendous joy he felt. It was not quite as easy for his wife, who would have painted this wonderful news in mile-high letters!

However, the fact remained under wraps until the press release early in December.

Martin received the award on 21st February, 1978, joining only 99 other holders of this prestigious award.

The President, Lord Aberconway, said of Martin:

"I have often felt rather apprehensive when watching Mr. Drew setting up Hillier's stand on a Monday afternoon before a Show here, that it will not be finished in time. But it always is, and finished immaculately, and labelled perfectly — so nowadays I just admire the process with enjoyment and no misgivings. Mr. Drew has been with Hillier's for 37 years, all of his working life so far. First in the alpine section, then for 20 years in the herbaceous section, during which time he staged their herbaceous exhibits. But for the last eight years, Mr. Drew, you have staged all the firm's exhibits, except when, as not infrequently happens in your firm, exhibits are being staged simultaneously at different shows, one perhaps overseas: for you can do most things except being in two places at once. For your exhibits you have had charge of the forcing and other preparation, of the plants. The number of Gold Medals won by those exhibits, Mr. Drew, must be matched by the amount of pleasure and admiration and knowledge you have afforded to all."

Martin met so many wonderful people in the course of his career including Royalty, politicians, sportsmen and stars of stage and screen. He so enjoyed talking with them all but above and beyond such pleasure was the camaraderie with colleagues from other firms. There was mutual respect, courtesy and kindness. A complete absence of friction, of variance. In fact, a true mateyness existed and Martin was happy to be part of this.

His work was widely reported in both local and national press and their tributes to his work, paint a clear picture of his incredible skill.

It's a golden oldie

er and Sons, of Winches-
ere among the exhibitors
15 European countries at
ecial international flower
in Italy, which finished
Sunday. And they came
with £500 worth of prizes.
re than half a million at-
d the show, which covered
enty-acre site at Genoa,
ised by the Association
nationale Des Producteurs
'Horticulture.

liers displayed more than
plants, comprising 720
ies and varieties worth
. They included rhodo-
rons, az...
y other shrubs,
space A face to look out for on the
rc feet. Hillier stand at nearly thirty
e plant major horticultural shows
n Winch throughout England this year
culated is that of showman and plantsman
Mr. Martin Drew.

was as far back as 1917 when
hrub of *Rosa hugonis* received
Award of Merit, and judging
ts condition on Hilliers Large
d Medal display it will still
round for many more years

th its fern-like foliage
h takes on a bronzed
arance in the autumn and
undance of pale yellow
rs followed by small dark
und fruits, it makes a
all-round shrub.
s is a fine shrub f
ers with restrict
' said experienced H
dener Martin Drew.

Martin Drew
with *Rosa
hugonis* in full
ower on
illiers
splav

A ROYAL BOUQUET FOR SHOWMAN MARTIN

MARTIN GOES FOR GOLD

ner ir
ibitions
Drew,
he sho
displa
Illiers
zes fe
oaks
thre
con
arded
ee th
the
nts 'perfection.

Martin is the man who is
primarily responsible for
staging the beautiful displays of
Hillier trees, shrubs and plants
which have won almost countless
gold medals, trophies and other
awards. He travels literally
thousands of miles every year,
nursing his plants and sometimes
working far into the night to
ensure that they are artistically
presented at the peak of

he was made an Associate of
Honour of the Royal Horticultura
Society and his presence on
Hillier's gold

Martin Drew

And at last the man be-
hind their success, ex-
hibitions manager, Mr.
Martin Drew, has pick-
ed up his own award.
He has been made an
Associate of Honour of
the Royal Horticultural
Society, one of the
society's highest awards.

Martin has been with the
firm for 30 years and
lives a stone's throw
head offices
Road, Win-

medals and two silver
medals.

He has also been involved
in the firm's success at
Chelsea Flower Show
where they have won
gold medal every ye
since the Second Wor
War.

His responsibility
beyond arranging
plants and flower
the firm's display
also has to ensur
are timed to reac
peak on show da
The final eal of
for his skills h
an invit
exh

TENDER PLANTS CAN BE TOUGH

ARE we missing out o
beautiful plants beca
think they are tender,
many of them can take
climate far better
know?
This was a point
Martin Drew, show m
Hilliers (Winchester)
Ltd. He included a
plant with a long n
exhibit — *Abutilon me
variegatum*, which i
thought to be tende
Martin was given
his own garden in
and it stood out all
its pot in the border
be planted, withou
and without harm w
flowering as we
those on show.
It has brig
foliage, yellow
the red and ye
Chinese lante
anthers pee
neath.
It comes
probably w
tender, bu
this to be
plant ju

SINGLE GOLD ANOTHER HONOUR FOR HILLIERS

Only a single Gold M
was awarded at the
Spring Show of the Royal
ticultural Society, held
week at the Old Hall, W
minster, and that was
Hillier Nurseries, of V
chester.

Their 170 square foot disp
was staged by Hilliers' S
Manager Mr. Martin Drew
resi t of the Greenhill
tric ster, who trav
lite of m
ea ge awa
wi of Hillie
tr at ma
s Britain (a
c eas).

Hilliers for Italy

Hilliers of Winchester w
representing the UK at the Eur
exhibition in Genoa, Italy, this
with a 91 sq m display bro
together at short notice.
It was at the end of January
the organisers of the exhibition
which begins tomorrow — ask
Hilliers whether they could stage
display following the sudden
drawal of another exhibitor.
The task was given to Mr Martin
Drew, well-known for his
displays at Chelsea and at t
Westminster shows
for the pur
treatme fro

Busy days
-what with
helsea
nd that
urth-floor garden

Martin Drew

Selfridges bursting into bloom
eir garden exhibition and Chelsea
Show opening its gates on
, to my mind the hero of the
Mr Martin Drew.
Drew has been organising
ons for the huge Hilliers Nurseries
hester for over 25 years and last
caught up with him

creations. This year the Harkne
was especially spectacular, as it
firm's centenary. It featured one
favourite little Polyantha roses,
White Pet which, suitable enough,
a hundred years old this year.
New introductions were the
yellow and red hybrid tea called

Left: Royal Horticultural Society's Spring Show at Westminster.

MORE GOLD MEDALS FOR HILLIER'S.

Below: Harrogate.

Above: Roy Lancaster and Martin with their Hillier exhibit at the Chelsea Flower Show. It won a Gold Medal! Below: The Rothschild Challenge Cup for Rhododendrons had eluded Hillier's and so there was tremendous rejoicing in the family and the firm when Martin won it in 1973 – and again in 1976 (this winning exhibit shown below).

Martin, Buckingham Palace and the Chestnuts!

Martin would often chuckle over one entry in his personal telephone directory — that of Buckingham Palace. He went there once a year to collect a sackful of conkers!

He would 'phone and make arrangements to meet the Queen's gardener and they would collect these special fruit of the Indian chestnut (Aesculus indica).

Harold Hillier had originally obtained these plants for the King and Queen (George VI and Queen Elizabeth, who is now our much loved Queen Mum). An avenue of 50 trees were planted at Buckingham Palace. On planting they were 12ft. to 15ft. high. They were spaced 20ft. apart, allowing for the enormous girth they would produce. Even so, it was decided to take out every other tree after 20 years to allow for the further space they would require.

The two trees that bore most of the fruit were those planted by the King and Queen and it was from these that Martin collected the conkers for propagation.

When he was exhibiting at the R.H.S. Show at Westminster, he would take a taxi, to and from, Buckingham Palace and the sack would then be transported back to Winchester, together with Martin's show plants.

The reason for the popularity of this variety of chestnut is its later flowering season and also the slender wood which prevents limbs breaking off under the weight of leaves, as so often happens with the normal horse chestnuts.

The Queen Mother

This story would be incomplete if it failed to mention Martin's great love and respect for the Queen Mother. Of all the members of our Royal Family, he found in her a true kindred spirit in the world of plants. Hers was not a polite interest but a knowledgeable and questioning one and Martin was honoured to meet her many times and was delighted when she actually recognised him on these occasions at Chelsea, Westminster and Sandringham.

Hillier's themselves were greatly honoured when, on behalf of Hampshire County Council, the Queen Mother accepted the Arboretum, an incredible gift from Hillier's to the world of Horticulture.

The Queen Mother with Sir Harold Hillier at the Arboretum at Braishfield.

Her Maje

talking to Martin.

Faking gardens for TV!

The BBC were to make a television play of the celebrated thriller of the '30s, 'Malice Aforethought', in which Hywell Bennett was to star as Dr. Edmund Bickleigh. A house at Micheldever was chosen as the location for much of the filming and Hillier's were given the task of relating the garden to the 1930 era. This was quite a challenge as varieties of plants had to be carefully chosen ensuring that they would have enhanced the gardens at that time and not have been introduced to the horticultural world during the intervening years.

Old looking walls were produced from polystyrene, with moss and lengths of ivy, deftly glued to produce the required effect. The tennis court was centre stage for important scenes, so much attention was given around this area.

This was a much enjoyed experience for Martin and none of the background work was lost on him, for he appreciated that even more than the end result.

Martin was a man of many and varied interests with the underlying theme being skill of the most intricate kind and incredible patience.

He liked crosswords, word puzzles and even jig-saws. He was no action man and although he loved watching cricket, left the necessary athleticism to those he felt more able!

His interest in aircraft continued throughout his life. As young men, Martin and Peter (his friend from Compton School) would set off on Peter's motorbike for the annual Farnborough Air Show. His interest was in the design and performance of these incredible machines and he had the ability to retain the facts and figures, the specification associated with each craft. He was able to identify by sound, and how he enjoyed the new phenomenon and so called 'sound barrier'.

Philately — one word and a powerful one that opened up a new world for Martin.

Martin was in his element when, in a roundabout way, he came to know Leslie Thomas (of *The Virgin Soldiers* fame). Leslie, himself one of the busiest of all busy men, has a great interest and even greater knowledge of stamp collecting. Martin, with his brother-in-law, John Barber, enjoyed his visits to Leslie and found, in him, one of the most fascinating characters he had ever encountered.

It was late in his own life that Martin first met this extraordinary man. His meeting with Leslie Thomas was undoubtedly, a highlight in his life and as Martin had the ability to savour enjoyment in retrospect, Leslie afforded him many pleasant hours.

Roy Lancaster – a great friend of Martin.

75

John Hillier presenting Martin with a barometer at Lady Hillier's home. Martin's colleagues at Hillier's also paid tribute to his work by buying and presenting him with a barometer, a great improvement on the Scarlet Pimpernel that had been his weather guide as a child.
Below: Martin on a wild flower hunt with his daughters, Elaine and Sarah, and Roy Lancaster and David Murray.

Margaret.

This photograph was taken a few years ago at Compton School by the school photographer. It was the photograph that Martin always carried with him (at least a smaller version of it).

The Last Chapter
by Margaret Drew

It is difficult to record this last chapter of Martin's life.

Martin left home on a fine November morning to attend the Royal Horticultural Society show at Westminster — a show he loved and one where he would meet up with friends and colleagues, immersing himself in the world of plants. He was looking forward to a happy day with people he held in high esteem and who, unreservedly, reciprocated his feelings.

This was the last show Martin would ever attend, indeed the *very* last time he would walk and talk.

On the way home, after leaving the train, he suffered a cruel stroke. It was a vicious major assault on Martin's body that left him helpless on the pavement of Winchester's Jewry Street.

His wife and daughters awaiting his homecoming received instead a call from the casualty department of Winchester Hospital.

The prognosis was hopeless. Martin's future had gone and, with it, the happy days of retirement he had worked so hard for. There was no way back to health, no way forward for living. He was taken to Clarke Ward and the beginning of the last incredible year of his life.

Anne (the Sister) and her staff (both nursing and non-nursing) were incredibly kind to all patients, showing the right degree of caring, producing a balanced cocktail of kindness, sympathy, flexibility and inflexibility peppered with the necessary taste of authority! It was the relatives, rather than the patients who were encouraged to imbibe themselves of this clever blend of encouragement and restraint.

Clarke Ward was, and still is, a busy medical haven for really sick people and was to become Martin's home for the next six months.

The prodigious work of the Consultants was humbling to witness . . .

Sadly, for some patients the bridge between sickness and health was just too long, making the journey forward an impossible one.

This was to be the case for Martin and for Gordon, a very dear man who shared those special days on the balcony of Clarke Ward, whilst his wife, Esther, and I shared our hopes and prayers for the recovery of our dear husbands.

Martin's first month in hospital was spent in the tiny side ward where it was thought, by some, that he would slip quietly away. We loved him so and here he was so gravely ill.

We (the girls and I) refused to listen to the voice of reason for very little is ever achieved by clear reason alone, because in any battle it remains firmly on the opposite side of faith and faith was our only hope.

As the reader will have concluded, Martin never hurried to do anything (as mentioned by Lord Aberconway at the award ceremony some ten years or so earlier!). Therefore the attitude of his wife, which she found quite natural to take, was that he would take his own time in which to recover.

He possessed the gift of patience and he possessed it in abundance but for now, he was entirely dependent upon the nursing skills of a group of dedicated young women. Chris who was on night duty when he was admitted to their care; Melanie, his primary nurse; Andrea (with the bow!), his senior nurse, and Sally and Lizzie. There were so many others who briefly touched his life and played such a vital part in the closing months. Together with them were Judy, Andrea, Denise and Lisa for although part of another team they too nursed Martin with such compassionate commitment.

Natalie, Annie and Haley provided the sustenance that was as necessary to survival, as a lifebelt to a drowning man. The many cheering cups of tea and coffee were wonderfully welcome and gave me the necessary impetus to meet each day.

The dedication and good humour that binds the Clarke Ward team together speaks volumes for the true professionalism of Anne (the Sister).

Time stretched itself to an unbearable length that first miserable lonely night that I spent at his side and found, for the first time ever, that I was unable to reach him. I could touch him, kiss him. But in his deep sleep, could he feel, did he know? Was this sleep, the prelude to death? Was Martin already beyond us, a step ahead.

There were no answers as the night slowly ticked away. I was very afraid in the darkness and yet had no desire for daylight to herald the start of tomorrow. It was more comfortable to be suspended in time but Time itself took on an authority I did not welcome for with its passing, the measure of recovery reached unknown depths.

Against my will, dawn pushed the night away and I was face to face with the cold hard light of the most unwelcome day of my life.

Martin was seriously ill, that was the uncompromising fact that stared me in the face and staring back in disbelief didn't frighten it away.

The work of the ward started in earnest, as the daily routine got underway and this brought a certain normality back into life.

Martin's garden at his home.

The Consultants were due soon, which was enough to cause the extra bustle. First through the door came John, and this filled me instantly with a calm, suppressed optimism. Martin had met this consultant before, albeit briefly, and held him in high esteem. I knew that Martin admired and respected John, and the girls and I totally trusted him.

The outside world came back into focus with the arrival of Dorothy Highfield. She stayed with me in Sister's office whilst another Consultant made his examination. He was totally honest and gave me no false hopes or promises.

Time was playing tricks on me. I had been at Compton School with Dorothy less than 24 hours earlier and yet another lifetime had passed in between. I could no longer comprehend the measurement of night and day. No longer did I understand life and death, and the heartbreaking 'in between'.

My brother, John, arrived soon after and I began to realise that hospital life and the world outside were about to blend.

Martin held on. Life was not discontinued; there was a pause. Was this the closing down of his being or merely an interruption? He was in the womb of time. Would it give birth to a future for him? Could we begin to look forward? There were no answers.

His wife and daughters began looking ahead, for to stand still was destructive.

The whole visible world was on the move as a river flowing. The movement was reality but the changing forms were only briefly with us. So we allowed ourselves to be carried along acknowledging a much changed, but nevertheless living, breathing Martin.

It would be wrong to say, as I overheard casually observed, that he was nothing but a shell of his former self.

He was beyond words, yet not beyond thought and his thoughts were mirrored in the one eye that opened, signalling his love of life and conveying his plea for a future.

Would it be possible to stem the tide and allow the future a chance?

Our friends poured in, to help.

The friendship we received was magnificent, as one by one they visited Martin.

Joy, Donna and Jill, from the Garden Centre opposite the hospital, came frequently with flowers and plants and the gardening chatter that would be familiar to the active brain of their colleague, if only a way could be found to penetrate the damage caused by the stroke and reach the Martin who was still there. He really was still there, as witnessed by my friend, Dorothy Angell, who came and asked a gardening question to which Martin responded with a shake of his head and then verified his response with a nod.

The days slipped by towards Christmas, the magical time of the year that meant so much to Martin. We hoped that the spirit of this season would prove strong enough to pull him right back into our world.

Martin left the side ward and moved to a bed beside the Christmas tree.

Following the Queen's speech on Christmas morning, the hospital radio broadcast a message from Roy Lancaster which brought tears to our eyes. Roy was so generous in his comments about Martin and there is no doubt they reached him as did the love so in evidence all around us.

In order to include Martin in the festivities, Sister agreed to let Nurse Emma gently brush the inside of his mouth with a swab moistened with sherry!

Boxing Day brought a visit from Dorothy Highfield and her daughter, Katherine. There are occasions in life when you recognise something special in another human being. Something that lifts them out of the general mass of humanity. Martin had seen this in Katherine. So he would have greatly appreciated her presence on one of the days of Christmas.

There were so many visits from friends, workmates, and old school mates. All tried to reach Martin. Sadly he remained a prisoner, locked in his damaged body.

I do not believe that I ever lost hope, although the icy chill of desperation was taking hold, and an unfriendly companion it proved. I looked for re-assurance. I wanted to find people who had suffered and recovered from similar strokes. I felt that someone, somewhere, must have the key to a magic ingredient. I felt like stopping the world. Calling all agencies to aid Martin. He shouldn't be left behind; they must wait. Someone, somewhere must have an answer.

Clutching at straws, I wrote to Raine Spencer, knowing that Earl Spencer had recovered from a serious stroke. She answered immediately, saying that the drug they obtained from Germany was for the pneumonia that set in afterwards and not for the stroke. She told me there was only hope and prayer — and urged me not to give up.

There was no way I could ever give up. I would push back the shadows that were gathering across our life together. Martin would have many tomorrows. The sun would pierce the morning mists and Martin would go out into the countryside once again. Admission is free, to the beauties of nature for a country boy like Martin.

Gordon left the balcony to go to another hospital where sadly on Easter Monday he died. Our hearts went out to Esther.

We held Martin's hand tighter, becoming increasingly aware how delicate was the thread that held our lives.

Martin with Ricky Dorlay, Dave Kemish and Andy Wright.

Not a single day passed without a visit from one or more of our friends. I started to write their names in a little notebook for Martin to see when he was well again. We believed it really showed how special he was, that friends should care so much and we felt truly blessed.

A most special person in Martin's life was Dave Kemish. They had worked together for many years, sharing hopes and impossible dreams and enjoying much laughter. Countless times they worked well into the night to ensure a particular 'show' would hit the road on time and many more times they had left Winchester in the early hours of the morning . . . they travelled hundreds of miles across the countryside, sometimes with Ricky Dorlay, in search of more awards that would proclaim 'their' firm, the best.

In Dave, Martin found a true friend and was delighted to attend his marriage to Wendy, who worked in Hillier's office.

Cicero wrote, many years ago that 'Life is nothing without friendship'. How true that remains today.

At this point I make no apology for recalling yet another gem from that same incredible philosopher. One that I feel to be truly apt.

In a letter to his son, Cicero wrote:
'But among all the methods of enriching oneself, there is no one better, no one more profitable, and pleasant, and agreeable, no one more worthy of a man and a gentleman, than that of manuring and tilling the ground.'

Jill and Cliff Thorne came many times and I especially welcomed their visits as Cliff was one person to whom Martin responded. Having suffered so much himself, he had that special insight that only deep suffering can give.

Sometimes Pat Hickman would come with Jill. Undoubtedly, Martin enjoyed their fun and laughter, reminding him of the time we all lived in Compton and certainly reminding me of the tea parties Jill, Pat, Helen and I had with our friend 'Mussey'.

When Roy Lancaster visited, his distinctive voice must surely have pulled Martin back into the world of plants for a while. It is in this world that Martin was most at home — the world of colour, of scent, of passion and of tenderness; a beautiful, gentle world in which we should all spend more time.

Jackie, a colleague of Sarah, sent many posies of sweet smelling flowers and shrubs for Martin to enjoy and there was none with a fragrance more powerful than that of *Daphne Jacqueline Postill*, a lovely shrub named after her by her husband, Alan.

The time for decisions was approaching.

Martin could not occupy the acute bed on the busy ward indefinitely. I knew, therefore, that it was right for him to come home. It was an easy decision to reach. Putting it into practice was far more difficult.

At this stage, our local surgery at Twyford entered the fray, full of enthusiasm. The wonderful support of Bruce, our doctor, and Joy, Jill and Carolyn, our district nurses, never faltered and we owe them much gratitude. They were ably backed by all surgery staff who, with cheerfulness and promptness, were to despatch many prescriptions in our direction.

Preparations were started. Elaine, Sarah and I changed the house around, discarding all unnecessary furniture in order to accommodate Martin's hospital bed and equipment.

We attended meetings with both Liz and Nick*, who had our welfare and well-being at heart by ensuring that we knew exactly what we were undertaking, whilst fully appreciating the forthcoming change in our lives. They realised, more than most, that the pattern of our lives would be different from anything we had ever known and made me accept that I could not allow my vision of life to be clouded by a false sense of self-sufficiency. I could not possibly be independent and I needed to accept all the help that was offered, for Martin's sake.

As far as the girls and I were concerned, we were to become a family once more. The house would again become home. Martin would be in our midst — and we gave heartfelt thanks that it was not yet time to say goodbye.

The hospital started to talk of a homecoming date.

You may remember the earlier reference of our 34th Wedding Anniversary.

This day now occupied my mind and I asked if it could possibly be arranged for Martin to come home before then in order for us to spend, for the first time ever, our Wedding Anniversary together.

Sadly, it was also to be for the last time.

I was blissfully unaware of that fact as the hospital pulled out all stops to finalise arrangements. There were so many changes looming. Not least taking my leave of the school where I had worked for over 20 years. This same village school, nestling at the foot of the Downs in the shadow of the old Norman church, that had played so great a part in the life of Martin and his family.

Here, in school, I saw the true value of human beings in the measure of their love transferred into thoughts, words and deeds. The Headmistress is blessed with exceptional understanding and had supported me tremendously during Martin's illness. My work colleagues propped me up daily and the kindness of Liz, Janet, Carol and Vi knew no bounds. It flowed like the river at Shawford, gently, calmly and eminently trustworthy.

(* Elizabeth Whetman, social worker, and Nicholas Black, clinical psychologist, both attached to the County Hospital, Winchester.)

At last the day of Martin's homecoming . . . We tied balloons to the gatepost and waited for the ambulance to arrive.

Martin was home again. Life was complete. I knew peace for the first time in months.

Elaine, Sarah and I felt such joy and gratitude. As the ambulance men carried Mart through the door, I said "You're home again, Marty" and he cried.

Time was absolutely meaningless at first. Day and night, as measures of passing life, ceased to exist. We ignored the time the world was living by and adopted our own survival clock, which stopped two-hourly for attention to be given to Martin.

Our First Wedding Anniversary — Together!

19th May dawned, heralding a bright clear day for our Anniversary. The memories of our wedding came flooding back, so long ago and yet just a yesterday. Such memories have no cash value and yet are priceless. They are the means whereby the past survives the present. During the afternoon Anne and Chris called to see us, bringing the good wishes of Clarke Ward. Looking at them, I realised I owed this special day to them and their colleagues and felt humble at the chance I had been given and had no intention of wasting it.

The following day Dorothy and Peter Highfield with Carol Moreton-Williams arrived, bringing a beautiful colour television set, a gift from the staff and children of Compton School. It was a wonderful, generous gift. The love and friendship that had prompted it gave us such strength and overwhelming peace in the knowledge that we were not alone in our fight for Martin.

After a few weeks, a true miracle arrived in the form of our greatly treasured Pegasus mattress. This was an incredible piece of equipment arranged for us by my sister-in-law, Patricia Barber, and it completely revolutionised our lives.

Martin benefited enormously from the gentle continuous therapy provided by the airway activity which prevents capillary occlusion and stimulates bloodflow. The bed sore he had left hospital with began to heal and eventually cleared completely. Although he was unable to move, Martin suffered no soreness or even reddening of the skin. This mattress pushed away the two-hourly boundary of our lives, and night and day returned.

The girls and I became adept at lifting and turning Martin and one or other of them would come home during their lunch time to help 'sit' him right up. Martin had no sitting action, as such. However, by means of deftly placed pillows he could be made comfortable in a semblance of that position.

Christopher, the Plant Centre Manager, was incredibly kind throughout and I knew a 'phone call was all that was necessary for Sarah to be allowed home to help in whatever way was needed. This took an enormous strain off of me and much worry evaporated. I was beginning to thoroughly enjoy having Martin at home and I knew he was happy.

I must pay tribute to the colleagues of both Elaine and Sarah. Their understanding did so much to turn what might have become a burden into a pleasure caring for a very sick but truly loved husband and father.

Summer came and our garden was a riot of colour. Flowers in profusion, all complementary, all in harmony. There was no discord. The herbaceous border reminded me of an orchestra just waiting for the hand of their conductor.

We longed to get Martin into his garden. He was a prisoner in his body; we were extending that misery by imprisoning him indoors.

Sadly, the wheels of officialdom seemed to move slowly and although a ceiling hoist and a wheelchair had been approved, they were locked in the system. Despite many hearty slaps on the back from our District Nurse Joy, in an attempt to get them 'coughed up', they remained stubbornly buried in paperwork.

At this stage, I wrote to the Royal Hospital and Home at Putney and count myself extremely fortunate to have been put in touch with Karen, a physiotherapist. What a sheer delight it was to speak with her. Her cheerfulness was infectious and her optimism equalled mine. She gave me much help and advice and became really determined that Martin should once again get out into his garden.

With this in mind, our friend Ben put up a pergola at the end of the garden and my brother, John, paved the area beneath, in readiness for the wheelchair. Sarah planted scented climbers that would cover the rustic poles, to give shade from the sun and a delightful fragrance for Martin to enjoy.

There were now definite signs of improvement and it was obvious that Martin understood what was said to him and he could respond in a limited way.

He was still unable to swallow so suffered the continual misery of feeding through a nasal gastric tube. At the suggestion of Pippa (a speech therapist), we began trying small pieces of food wrapped in muslin, the ends of which we firmly held. Martin chewed and enjoyed the flavour of various foods, including sausage and chips (always a favourite) that my friend, Dorothy Angell, brought one day.

The girls and I exercised his limbs frequently and rotated his joints. He was not impressed by this! In any case this would have been his normal response to unnecessary exercise (even though the effort was all ours).

By now his other eye had opened. So I brought down our long mirror from upstairs which Ken Angell kindly fixed to the wall at the bottom of the bed. Consequently, Martin could see the whole room and even the post box outside the front garden.

Both eyes moved independently so that he was able to look in two different directions at one and the same time. I was worried as to how much Martin could actually see and whether perhaps he was having double or blurred vision. An eye test was essential and an optician sought. This proved to be more easily said than done, for despite the continual efforts of our District Nurse Joy and myself there was no such provision under the National Health Service.

We contacted the premises of Winchester opticians and all confirmed they no longer made home visits for eye examinations. They did furnish us with the name of a retired optician who was prepared to come privately. This was arranged and was the source of much amusement to Martin. The kindly gentleman arrived and stood his board, with letters of varying size, at the bottom of the bed. So far, so good but how, he wondered, could someone completely unable to speak indicate what letters he could see. He stood perplexed wondering whether indeed Martin could even see the board.

Suddenly, his voice cut through the vague uncertainty with "Nod if you can see my board" and Martin responded with a greatly exaggerated nod of his head, taking the optician completely by surprise and leaving him to reply somewhat lamely "He can see," to which Martin laughed heartily!

These flashes of humour never deserted Martin and were a delight.

He thoroughly enjoyed his usual comedy programmes on television and chuckled at radio humour whether the humour was intended or not. One instance of this was Jimmy Young interviewing Prime Minister Margaret Thatcher. She was making a firm point and her voice became more Maggie than Maggie as if she was drawing herself up to full height! Martin was delightfully amused and his laughter is something I will remember always.

It was not long after this that Margaret Thatcher resigned and Martin watched all the resulting controversy with real interest.

He had such a love of music, mainly instrumental. Doris and Peggy, our friends in Canada, dearly loved by Martin, sent many tapes for him to listen to and he enjoyed them all. They also sent various pieces of equipment, unavailable to us here but so necessary to Martin's comfort and wellbeing.

When the Postman knocked the door with a parcel from Canada I used to say "Let's see what Doris and Peggy have sent" as I opened it at his bedside. There were tears in his eyes as I added "They'll be home soon." They were but it was not to be soon enough for Martin.

Pippa (speech therapist) had organised an electric board on which various drawings and statements were shown. So that by lightly pressing on a pad,

Martin would move the arrow to point at any directive he wished to give — such as too hot, too cold, music, television, yes, no. Sarah drew pictures to accompany these statements and we moved them around the board so that every response was thought out and not automatic.

We also put pictures of flowers and shrubs around the board, asking Martin to point to certain ones, using their Latin names. He never got one wrong. He still knew his plants backwards!

A wonderful day for Martin was the arrival of Laurence Flatman and his wife, Doreen. Laurence works for Blooms of Bressingham, the great nurserymen based in Norfolk. They had met at shows all over the country. Martin liked and admired Laurence and found him to be a wonderful person. They became good friends and there is no doubt that Martin recognised the voice of Laurence and that it would have given him immense pleasure and quiet happiness. Although he was unable to express his joy at their visit, I know that it was there and would have given him happy, comforting thoughts knowing that Laurence and Doreen cared enough to come all this way.

Martin was gaining more control of his facial muscles and could raise his eyebrows and close his eyes when asked. He was also beginning to turn his head. He could wave goodbye — but only by moving the left arm from the elbow down. Nevertheless, he began to say goodbye in this manner frequently and almost always for Nurse Carolyn, a very pretty young lady!

Martin would surely recover

The harvest moon, illuminating the night sky, signalled that the time of thanksgiving was with us once again and now had to be extended beyond the thankfully received crops of the fields to the receiving of help and of love. One was nourishment for the body, the other for the soul and both vital to human life. Manna to sustain complete existence.

Our thanksgiving was total. For Consultants — John, Hugh and Andrew, Sister and staff of Winchester Hospital. Our family doctor, district nurses and staff of Twyford surgery. The Headmistress and all staff and children of Compton School. My very dear Dad, heading our family and truly wonderful friends and especially for my sister-in-law, Pat, as without the Pegasus mattress I doubt whether either Martin or I could have kept going so happily and so well.

Martin would surely recover, surrounded by so much love. I felt very content.

The month wore on to Hallowe'en and we decorated Martin's drip stand with a witch on a broomstick, causing much merriment to Nurse Carolyn when she visited Martin that day.

Our three district nurses had become firm friends and we looked forward to their visits. They were different in character but truly complemented each other. Initially they called in twice a day; within a week, we all realised this was unnecessary and a daily visit to dress Martin's bed sore was more than adequte. After a few months and the real signs of Martin's foot healing added to their growing confidence in my ability, their visits became reduced to alternate days. At the same time I was left in no doubt whatsoever that they were only a 'phone call away and I could ring day or night if there was a problem.

I will never forget the day that Joy called in and I gave Martin my kitchen spoon asking him to point to a welly boot on a page full of different objects. With the restricted movement of his lower left arm, the spoon wobbled towards the boots.

Joy looked at Martin and inclining her head to indicate me, said "She's thick, isn't she, Martin, if she doesn't know what a welly boot looks like?" Martin's laughter had Joy and I in tears.

Then we received a 'phone call from Karen, of the Royal Hospital and Home at Putney, saying she had permission to come down in a van with a technician, bringing a wheelchair to be fitted for Martin in our home.

Great joy! I told Martin that his days in the garden were not far away. I planned to take him back to Winchester Hospital to meet everyone who had looked after him. We would walk on the Downs and enjoy the autumn colours and the falling leaves.

I didn't sleep the night, following Karen's call.

Winchester were informed and they told Putney they would provide the chair; so it was agreed to leave it with them. As Karen observed, "So long as Martin gets his chair, it really doesn't matter who provides it."

Winchester Social Services came out to look again and to measure doors for ease of access and to look at the possible necessity of a ramp. There were no problems as the front door of the house was more than wide enough to accommodate a wheelchair and a ramp would not be needed. A ceiling hoist was promised in order that we would be able to swing Martin out of bed into his chair. But I began to realise that it would be snow, rather than autumn colours we would be going out to see!

After a chat together, the girls and I agreed it would be sensible to discard yet more furniture to make plenty of room for manoeuvring and for good measure, a little more, to leave enough space for a recliner chair so that Martin would be able to join the family circle once he could be lifted from his bed, the bed that was fast becoming his prison.

The recliner chair was ordered and arrived the following week. Still we awaited the hoist and the wheelchair.

Optimism

By now, optimism had gone to my head, and a powerful potent it proved to be!

We continued to enjoy daily visits from friends. So many true and loyal people. Muriel Richardson, whom I had known since she and I started and ran the Compton and Shawford Brownie Pack for 23 years, came most Saturdays. I welcomed her company as Martin had known her since her childhood days. He would have been quite comfortable and content in her presence.

November 28th approached. One year had passed since Martin's stroke. A year when we had experienced every emotion that existed and, I suspect, some that didn't! One year when life had become infinitely precious. A year not without its battles and many of them still to be won. A year that had shown us great love and kindness and loyalty, pessimism and optimism. A year of great contrasts but a year with Martin.

The days became shorter, as the lengthening hours of darkness began to squeeze out the daylight. There was a nip in the air. Winter was with us once again.

The birds were greatly attracted to the ripe orange berries hanging on the pyracantha outside the lounge window, in full view of Martin. When it rained, the berries glistened and drooped in their fullness. Their seductive ripeness proved irresistible to our feathered friends, who soon made short work of our only remaining autumn colour.

The grey days of winter were banished by the firelight flickering across the ceiling and the count-down to Christmas had begun.

We started decorating a little earlier in order for Martin to enjoy it over a longer period. Sarah took charge of the tree and it was placed just left of the foot of his bed. He watched her, as she added white candles, red bows of ribbon and red and gold baubles. Looking at his dear face, I wondered what he was feeling as the decorating of Christmas trees past had been left exclusively to him.

His artistic flair coupled with his feeling for the Christmas festival was brought to bear on this labour of love and the result symbolised the simple shining beauty of this special time of the year. For in past years once he had completed decorating the tree, he turned his thoughts to the post box outside the house. Having asked the GPO for permission to adorn their old familiar red box with tinsel and artificial snowflakes, he then managed to arrange a star to shine above it. The glittering star 'caught' all the headlights and shone out from the darkness, like a diamond on black velvet. This was achieved under the cloak of nightfall with his family, persuaded willing accomplices, holding torches!

91

Somehow, we now had to manage this without him and doing the best we could, had to acknowledge our defeat with the star. We did, however, accomplish his usual Christmas scene in the porch, using another tree this time decorated with all the spare ornaments collected over the years; each one bringing a 'do you remember when . . .' to the proceedings.

Christmas records were played over and over again, losing nothing in the repetitive rendering. In fact, those sung by Winchester Cathedral Choir were enhanced by their familiarity.

So many friends popped in to bid us a happy Christmas with none more welcome than workmates Tom Long, Ben Maskell and Geoff Knight. Martin had known them many years and truly valued their friendship. Between them they clocked up quite a few decades with Hillier's, certainly well over 100 years of loyal dedicated service, the like, of which, made this firm great.

The magic of Christmas Eve was heightened by the sound of children's voices singing outside.

The joy and expectancy of the season added a sweetness to their youthful sounds guaranteed to tug at heartstrings. Our emotions, already fragile, were able to respond to the goodwill all around as we opened the door to find our dear friends Jan and Steve Murray with the children, Heather, Vicky, Lyndsay and Mark, who excitedly tumbled in.

They were so good with Martin. Although respecting his illness, they spoke to him quite normally. No hushed or diffident tones peppered their chatter. Martin was still Martin who, sadly, was poorly. They remained their open honest selves and there was no embarrassment. I loved them for that.

They added their gifts to the growing pile beneath the tree. Parcels wrapped in an assortment of colours, tied with bows and streamers, bearing love, friendship and caring in its many forms.

As Christmas Eve drew to a close, a gentle hush blanketed the world. Problems were put on hold as we soaked up the peace that abounds.

The spirit of goodwill is for all mankind and we felt it with us as we said goodnight on the eve of Christmas Day.

My dear Dad who had come to spend the holiday with us, went early to bed. He had been such a tremendous support during Martin's long illness and backed us wholeheartedly in every move we made. His unquestioning support has always been there for all of his children with wisdom enough to allow each to make their own mistakes and profit from the learning. The old adage of being unable to put old heads on young shoulders is as true today as it ever was, and he had the foresight to realise this.

He had spent the previous Christmas with us, when we had indeed been a family divided. Divided by the uncomfortable breach of illness. There had been no way of avoiding the feeling of isolation, of entering no man's land. Now we were all together again.

Christmas Day dawned early for us, as we made Martin comfortable in readiness for opening the traditional Christmas stockings and unwrapping the assortment of exciting parcels illuminated by the gentle glow of the Christmas lights.

I opened Martin's on his bed so that he might see and feel everything he'd been given — and what an assortment! Toiletries of every conceivable description, some especially smart pillowcases for his bed and a lovely creamy yellow honeycomb blanket. Records of favourite music and gardening books for the future. A striking Mathew Norman carriage clock that I had saved up to buy from the little antique clock shop in Winchester's Cathedral Square, knowing how Martin would delight in this at his bedside.

And from the children who had sung carols just the evening before, a lovely china dish which on it, written in gold lettering, said 'Margaret and Martin, with love at Christmas'. A gift I shall treasure, for I will never be able to receive its like again as now there is no Martin.

Suddenly and without warning on Christmas afternoon, he died. He died before our family doctor and the ambulance could get here, although they arrived within minutes. He died despite our pleas of "Hang on, Martin". He died despite our prayers and despite our love.

How poignant that the delicate thread that held his life should break on the one day in all the year, he loved so much.

Dad took over and 'phoned my brother and sister knowing the sad news would be passed to all the family once Christmas Day was over.

We had no wish to sadden them earlier than necessary. Nevertheless we were much comforted by the arrival of my brother and sister-in-law. They travelled from their home to us, leaving my nieces Kate and Jaclyn with Pat's parents. They came to offer support and sympathy and their kindness did much to calm and comfort us all, as we realised we were not alone in our overwhelming distress.

Unbelievably, it was still Christmas Day. So much had happened. It couldn't be true. It mustn't be so.

I felt the shadow that had fallen across my life would not fade with the dying sun. It would blight even the darkness.

We were all numb, anaesthetised. The well worn platitudes of 'being at peace' and 'now somewhere better' irritated me and were far more painful than salt rubbed into an open raw wound.

I felt Martin had been cheated. He had faithfully completed the hard work of life and been denied the fruits this labour should bear.

During the following days, dozens of letters dropped through the letter box, paying tribute to Martin, to his work, to his life. His greatness had been his simplicity.

On 3rd January, 1991 at Compton Church, friends and relatives gathered to pay their last respects.

It was a beautiful moving service with Dorothy Highfield (Headmistress of Compton School) reading the poem 'Peace' and Roy Lancaster giving the address.

Roy spoke warmly of Martin and of his expression, "Well, what do you reckon?" and concluded by saying "We shall all miss him as will the horticultural world in general. But you know, he was such a character and I shouldn't be at all surprised if he is up there right now staging yet another exhibit and asking his new employer — 'Well, what do you reckon?'.''

With the very kind permission of the Rector, that saying of Martin's is now engraved on his headstone in the little churchyard adjoining the school and the church.

John Hillier has promised that the firm of Hillier's will plant a hedgerow of small trees and shrubs along the boundary of the school, bordering Compton Street, as a living Memorial to Martin and work has already begun with the parents of today's schoolchildren, joining together in the preparation.

And so, as the sun sets at the end of each day with the promise of a new dawn, we must remember that a truly beautiful new dawn has now broken for Martin. Far more beautiful than he has ever known before. More beautiful than we are able to contemplate.

We must not allow our own private pain and heartbreaking grief to cast shadows over his everlasting peace.

God bless Martin, a true country boy and worthy village lad.

P.S.

Headmistress Dorothy Highfield and volunteers (left to right: Dick Nicholson, Tim Hunt, Dorothy Highfield, Terry Carter (at back), Bill Robinson, Peter Laver, George Medd, Graham Hill) during a break in their drive to clear the boundary areas around Compton School so that the firm of Hillier's can plant a hedgerow of small trees as a living memorial to Martin.